Success Signals:
A Guide to Reading
Body Language

By Patti Wood, M.A., C.S.P.

Success Signals: A Guide to Reading Body Language

© 2005 by Patti Wood

ISBN 0-9646338-6-6

For more information, contact

Communication Dynamics
2312 Hunting Valley Drive
Decatur, GA 30033
404-371-8228
www.pattiwood.com

Cover design by Sharon Powers

Interior book design and layout by Martha Nichols/aMuse Productions

Acknowledgments

I WOULD LIKE TO THANK ALL THE AUDIENCE MEMBERS AND TRAIN-ing class participants from my workshops, seminars and other events for asking great questions about body language.

Thanks to all my nonverbal communication instructors in undergraduate and graduate school. Your courses gave direction to my curiosity. To all the students in my body language and nonverbal communication courses both at Florida State and Oglethorpe Universities, thank you for your boundless enthusiasm for the class. Teaching you was one of my life's great joys.

Thanks to all the friends and clients over the years who said, "Where's the book?" especially Michael, Frank and Linda. To my family — Mom, Janice and Robin — thanks for being there for me. Pamela, thanks for your excitement in helping with the survey research.

Thanks to John Clark. You have an eye for detail and a great big heart. And to Steve Cohn who said the magic words, "It needs more stories," Thank you for you help, Steve, in releasing my natural voice.

Deep love and thanks to my to best friends Elaine Fuerst and Pat MacEnulty, the two most remarkable women I know. I am blessed to call you friends and soul sisters. Elaine, marketing guru extraordinaire, I am finally taking your advice: Here is the book!!! Thank you for believing in my ability. Pat, a brilliant writer, your support, editing services and prayers are the reason this book is possible.

Contents

INTRODUCTION

THE HEAD OF SALES SHIFTS TO THE RIGHT IN HIS CHAIR, THE project manager looks down and away and then taps his pencil, the finance person swallows and then coughs — all in response to the chairman's idea for cost savings. I am in a boardroom meeting watching these behaviors as a communication consultant. My job is to tell the chairman what's going on at the meeting and whether certain people are buying-in or tuning-out. I continue to watch each interaction, study all the body language and note the shifts in each person's voice. I then brief the chair.

Wouldn't you like to know what all the nonverbal behaviors mean? Wouldn't you like to know how to interpret accurately the nonverbal cues your customers, co-workers, friends, spouse, and anybody else in your life are giving? They say we can't read minds, but reading body language can give you insight into the minds and the hearts of everyone you interact with.

Wouldn't you like to be able to say, "I know what you're thinking..." and really know what they're thinking?

We have the ability to send out and read more than 700,000 different nonverbal cues. That's right — 700,000! While we spend large chunks of our lives learning how to read and write words, we miss the thousands of cues that come through the body and the nuances of the voice. And if you miss all that, what happens?

Nonverbal behavior affects everything

You know you don't come across well with strangers, but you don't know how to improve the impression you give. You think you understand what your boss wants, but you get it wrong.

You think you were clear with what you wanted and someone misreads you. You rush through a phone call to a friend and miss the cues that tell you she is unhappy and wanted to talk more. You're sitting in a meeting and you have great ideas but someone else always interrupts and talks over you. You're out with a group of friends and you miss the subtle cues that could make you shine. You fail in your romantic relationship and don't know why. And so much more.

Understanding nonverbal communication is essential if you want to succeed in anything you do, personally or professionally. Reading this book and doing the self tests and exercises can create a change in you that will make your life easier, make your work life more successful, and make your relationships with other people happier, warmer and more satisfying. And "seeing" what is not being said (verbally) is a lot of fun.

Why are there so many ways for us to communicate without words? Because we need them and have always needed them. From the first time we cry at birth, we have a need to be understood. When our parents hear our cries and see our smiles or our funny, pinched faces and kicking legs, they wonder what we're saying. Is it that we're hungry, in need of a diaper change or simply longing to be held? We cannot tell them with words, but we are speaking volumes nonverbally.

As we grow and learn language, we begin to rely on words, or verbal language, to get our message across to others. We spend years learning how to communicate through the spoken and written word. In school, our teachers labor with us over papers and books, and at home, our parents anxiously check our grades to judge our progress. Yet as adults, we often find it difficult to make ourselves understood, or we misinterpret the words of others and don't know why.

Understanding what others think, want and feel is essential to our success, as is getting others to understand us. So, what makes it so hard? What's missing?

What we're missing are the success signals of nonverbal communication.

We have forgotten or have ignored this nonverbal communication, even though it was the first language we spoke. We think if people hear our words, it's all we need to communicate. But what we lose is meaning. We miss the communication that comes from using space, touch, movement, gestures, objects, time, sounds and more. Understanding this secret language of success — our nonverbal body language and paralanguage (the nuances of the voice) — can help us communicate with others more effectively because that is how we show our truest, most honest thoughts and feelings.

There is a simple reason why this is true. Since nonverbal signals are not under our conscious control, our nonverbal communication gives a more honest and revealing message. So when you understand people's body language, you can effectively figure out their motivations, and most importantly, it allows you to see into their hearts. It allows you to have super powers.

Imagine. You are sitting in an interview for a job you really want. You notice that as the interviewer begins to talk with you, she seems slightly detached. While she's telling you all about the company and the job, her facial expressions tell you she has made this same speech several times before (which is probably true). Her eyes occasionally look over to her computer screen until you get the feeling she's more interested in her email than in you. After she asks you a general question about your experience, you begin to talk and she begins to listen, but you notice her legs are facing away from her desk and you. Suddenly, you lean forward, lower your voice and say, "my last boss gave me lots of freedom. By letting me come up with ideas and then letting me run with them … I saved the company 10 … million … dollars."

You finish the statement and notice her body straighten, her legs moving back under the desk towards you and her eyes focus on yours. You smile and sit back in your chair and say, "I think, with the right environment, I can do the same here." The interviewer looks at you for a moment, sits back in her chair and says, "Well, that's interesting. What about …" You know you have penetrated the veneer of control she had at the beginning of the interview. She may be trying to show she hasn't been persuaded, but you know by her nonverbal cues that you have made an impact. Later on, she says she still has others to interview, but she grips your hand tightly, smiles broadly and makes eye contact for longer than three seconds. Her words say, "We're not sure," but her nonverbal cues say, "When can you start?"

That's right, just like Superman, you can have a form of x-ray vision. Understanding body language is like having an agent 007, high-tech hearing device and access to a database of others' secret thoughts (which can be a little scary!).

You unlock these super powers when you bring your ability to read nonverbal communication up to your conscious control.

UNDERSTANDING THE MESSAGES YOU SEND

There's another and equally important aspect to body language and paralanguage — understanding the messages you are sending out to others. By looking at your own body language, you can find out what you're truly feeling and what messages you are transmitting.

Understanding body language gives us more than clarity — it gives us peace of mind. We feel tension when we don't understand other people's actions and motivations. We may not know where that tension is coming from, but we expend a lot of energy worrying and guessing about the motives of other people.

Understanding body language is about knowing yourself, your world and the other people in it. With this understanding, you can analyze your own body language cues and gain insight into why you may have been feeling sad or restless. You'll understand why you get a good feeling around one person and negative feelings around another. You'll get clarity on why you hired an employee who made you feel comfortable even though they had fewer qualifications than a candidate who made you feel ill at ease.

Some people might say that lifting the veil so we can see the truth in others' behaviors is a scary prospect. I don't think so. There was a line from an old radio show called The Shadow: "Who knows what evil lurks in the hearts of men? The Shadow knows." Well, the Shadow was just a really good body language expert. According to the old radio show, the Shadow had unusual insight into others' psyches that he used to fight evil. Would you like to have that insight? Learn about nonverbal communication — your own and others.

While we may not want to don a cape and fight crime, we can use our insights to uncover and even prevent deception and negativity. We can lift the veil to bring unspoken feelings to light, and that light can help us create more open and honest relationships.

In reality, lifting the veil usually shows us much more good than bad. One night I was telling some friends what I had gained from my insights in body language. I gushed about all the wonderful relationships I had made, the secrets they and I had revealed, and the special, almost holy bond you make with someone when you can see their true essence and allow them to see yours. One of my friends, who has known me for years said, "I always saw you as Pollyanna, the girl who saw the good in everyone!" Well, I do see the good — and you can, too.

Success Signals will help you illuminate your life situations through understanding body language and other nonverbal cues. It will help you understand the role of body language in your everyday interactions, from dating and choosing a mate, to finding the right job, selling yourself or your product, and dealing with employers and employees. You'll learn how your body language can bolster your self-confidence and credibility and how "reading" others' body language can help you spot deception. However, it's not about "catching" others. It's about communicating honestly. Understanding and using these techniques won't make it easier to fool other people, but it will enable you to communicate your thoughts, feelings and ideas more effectively and to understand what others are communicating to you.

In this book, you'll find self-evaluation tools, exercises, tips and techniques for understanding and utilizing body language and other forms of nonverbal communication, giving you insight into your personal and professional situations. You'll learn about gender differences, the importance of touch and ways to establish rapport. In addition to enriching your personal life, you'll gain greater understanding of the role body language plays in our diverse culture, giving you an edge in business situations.

Although other books deal with various aspects of body language and nonverbal communication, Success Signals also examines the relationship between body language and emotion. This book will show you how you can use body language to change the way you feel physically and emotionally and to affect the way others feel.

A HOLISTIC APPROACH

In this book and in the seminars and workshops that I conduct on nonverbal communication, I take a holistic approach to body language. Correctly interpreting nonverbal communication is never based on isolated behaviors, but in knowing how to read body language within a context and reading behaviors and expressions in the correct order. Through these techniques, you'll learn how to read the "whole body" and to take into account those other subtle indicators of attitude and emotions, such as context, punctuality, dress, and so forth, enabling you to make complete and accurate assessments.

Understanding the "success signals" of nonverbal communication will change the way you look at people and life. It is an adventure that few get to take.

Welcome aboard.

Nonverbal Communication Self-Test

Take this self-test to determine what you need to improve in your communication.

1. How do you think understanding and using nonverbal communication (body language and voice) can benefit you?
    a.
    b.
    c.

2. Which of the following would you most like to do?
    a. Improve your ability to read others
    b. Improve your own body language

3. Rate your ability to notice body language cues.

Poor	Fair	Good	Very good	Excellent
1	2	3	4	5

4. Rate your ability to read body language — that is, to understand what it means.

    How accurate were you? (Circle your answer.)

Not Accurate	Somewhat Accurate	Accurate	Very Accurate	Extremely Accurate
1	2	3	4	5

5. What is the biggest body language mistake that someone can make (that is, a mistake either in the way they behave or in the way they interpret others)?

6. What one body language behavior do you like least in others?

7. Is there a body language behavior you would like to change in yourself?
    a. ____Yes ____No
    b. If there is, what is it?

8. Briefly describe a time in your life when body language or voice caused a problem for you or someone else.

Chapter 1

What Are the Secrets
of Body Language?

"I never talk to our manager face to face."

"He always sends me emails instead of just coming to talk to me, and his cubicle is right next to mine!"

"He wears some kind of black sci-fi themed t-shirt everyday, even when customers are on site."

"He has taken a room divider from the conference room and put it across the opening to his cubicle, and he brought in a big piece of plastic and put a roof on it!"

"When he talks to you he never looks at you."

"He sits in his dark cave hunched over the computer, walled away from all of us like the Lord of the Rings *hobbit he wears on his shirt!"*

THESE WERE COMPLAINTS A TECH TEAM AT ONE OF THE HIGH-tech companies where I was a consultant made about their young manager. They had been under an enormous amount of pressure and had been overworked. They all complained that their manager rarely talked to them.

He sent them assignments via email, walked past them in the hallway with his head down and his hands in his pockets, and responded to visits to his cubicle as if they were invisible, not looking at them and continuing to type on the computer. If they dared interrupt his flow of thought in a meeting, he would give them a brief, pained look and keep talking really fast in an urgent whisper.

His employees weren't just irritated, they were mad. They felt he didn't care about them. The more they pushed to talk, the more he retreated. His behavior seemed bizarre. They ended up having no respect for him and consequently had very little motivation to perform well in their jobs.

What were the secret success signals that the employees where missing? Read the nonverbal cues once more. This time, look for the secret symbolic message common to all the cues. When you've done that, continue reading.

When I first started coaching this manager, he said, "I don't know what the big deal is. I get my work done. I don't have time to 'visit' all day and I don't want 'make friends' with my employees." He said he was too busy! He was too busy working to change things about his nonverbal communication that were dramatically affecting his work!

We went through a step-by-step process. We helped him become aware of the signals he was sending out and what they were communicating. We worked on improving his nonverbal output, as well help him read behaviors. As part of a self-evaluation process you will learn about in this book, he revealed the true reason for his behavior. Did you get the secret from his cues?

He was scared! He was retreating from close interactions because he did not know how to read people. He was hiding under his roof, wearing the protective color black, speeding through conversations, too scared to make eye contact. But his employees misinterpreted all those cues.

As I asked him about his life experiences, the reason became clear: he had spent his life in front of the TV, the computer, and his Game Boy®. Growing up, he ate dinner alone. In college, his social interactions were with his Internet pals. He had missed the critical years he needed to learn body language. Now as an adult, he could "get" the words in emails but all the subtle nuances of body language were a mystery. He was, in a word, clueless, and that made any face-to-face interaction scary. He was in a foreign land and he hadn't learned the language. After I coached him in the success signals of body language, this very smart hobbit became a great manager. Whether you are a hobbit or a people-savvy person who wants to up the bar on your interpersonal success, this book will help you.

Tip: The employees were responding emotionally to their manager's nonverbal cues; they didn't look deeper. When you feel strong emotions in response to someone, look for the deeper secrets in their communication. Take yourself out of the equation and ask yourself, "What could be going on with him that is causing him to act this way?"

Tip: *The manager was not getting what he wanted from his employees; he said he didn't have the time to fix it. But he was wasting far more time dealing with the negative undercurrent. When you are having interpersonal conflicts, take five minutes to talk face to face or as a fall back, on the phone to talk. The stress you save may be your own.*

So what are the benefits of body language?

Body language is revealing

The former hobbit discovered the power of body language and why it affects virtually everything we do and everything we want to accomplish. We communicate nonverbally through an enormous number of factors including territory, appearance, scent, accessories, artifacts, and even room design, color, time use and more. Our minds are constantly examining these various factors and translating what these behaviors might mean.

While you can consciously control your words, your nonverbal signals are not always under your conscious control, and they send a more honest and revealing message. From million-dollar business deals to first dates and family dinners, from assessing a politician to conversing with a friend, body language plays a major role in our happiness and prosperity.

With so many possible signals, nonverbal communication is more complex than verbal language. You can look up the meaning of a word in any dictionary, but to understand body language and vocal paralanguage (volume, tempo, and so forth) you need years of practice — or this book. The husband who can read his wife's shoulder shrug, her frown and her downcast eyes as she says, "Nothing's wrong," and knows to probe further because he senses that something is wrong, can have a happier spouse and a happier marriage. The sales representative who can tell when her prospect has lost interest in her presentation can shift her delivery and still close the deal.

Body language can change the way we feel

The brain physically affects your body language and sends the body messages telling it how to move and what to do. Conversely, the way you hold and carry yourself, your gestures, your movement through space and even your facial expressions send messages back to your brain. So if you stand with your shoulders drooping and head bowed, the little pharmacy in your brain creates negative chemicals in less than a fortieth of a second and sends them into your bloodstream to make you feel the way you look.

You probably have heard how runners get their "runner's high." The physical action of running sends messages to the brain that says, "I need my runner's high prescription filled so I can keep going." And the brain fills out the prescription. The same is true for you in your everyday life. Your body's messages send a prescription order to your brain. In Edgar Allen Poe's story The Purloined Letter, one of the characters tells the story of an eight-year-old boy who can always win at the game of odds and evens. In this game, someone holds a closed hand over some marbles and the other person must guess whether there is an even or an odd number of marbles. The boy had a theory about how people would behave, based on how smart or how stupid they were. He then explained that he could tell what the other person was thinking and know the other person's character simply by assuming the same facial expression. When he took on their facial expressions, he actually produced some of the same chemicals as they did and it was as if his mind worked in the same way as theirs did.

This is true in real life as well, as the saying goes: "Act as if and you will be." For example, let's say you are at a party or a big business meeting and you do not know anyone. Everyone else is dressed up in fancy clothes and you came in your jeans and buttoned-down shirt. You stand with your arms folded tightly in front of you, your legs close together while you bite your bottom lip with tension. You may be breathing fast with your chest going up and down. All these simple shifts in body language send a message to your brain, and the brain pharmacist says that this must be a bad situation — so he fills out a prescription for tense, nervous chemicals to stream into your bloodstream to make you feel more tense and tight.

Say you decide to act cool and calm in this situation even if you don't quite feel that way. You consciously stand relaxed, leaning against a wall. You uncross your arms, smile and breathe slowly, relaxing your chest. The pharmacist gets the message, and soon you really do feel calm.

Watch chess masters playing chess. They know to sit with their backs straight, and to lean forward aggressively. If they sit in a lethargic posture, their brains will be lethargic. If they sit like warriors, their brains will know that they are in battle.

We often think that we feel something and our body language reflects those feelings. You feel tired, your body slouches, your shoulders roll forward, and your head moves forward. The inverse is also true. You can hold your body in a certain way and begin to feel that way. You stand up straight, pull your shoulders back and pull your head back level with your shoulders, and you begin to feel alert. You can decide how you want to feel, match your nonverbal cues to the state you desire, and voila! You can change how you feel. Try smiling when you're feeling blue — see what happens. All those motivational speakers weren't wrong. It's hard to stay sad with a smile on your face.

The connection between body language and brain chemistry is great news. Learn what creates powerful body language messages, integrate that with an awareness of your own body language, and you can feel as powerful, happy or relaxed as you wish.

Business "goes better" with body language

You have so much to get done at work and at home so you put your nose to the grindstone and focus on your "to-do's." You have twelve-hundred-thousand emails you have to answer, 372 meetings to prepare for and a list of tasks to complete as long as your arm, leg, and nose. You might think, "If I work hard, success will be mine." Well, yes, that's somewhat true. But if you ever get your "to-do's" and tasks done (if that is your goal) and haven't paid attention to body language — your own and others' — reaching personal success will be a long time in coming.

Understanding body language can help business people determine others' motivations and analyze business interactions much more effectively than simple reliance on spoken words. Professionals who understand nonverbal cues can evaluate what their clients, customers and co-workers are really telling them in order to know how to better meet their needs — to give a better price, offer more (or fewer) details, give a more heartfelt, emotional message, wrap it up and go for the close.

For instance, in a sales setting, a prospect may be saying, "Yes, go on," but if her arms and legs are crossed with one foot bouncing towards the door, her nonverbal signals are sending a different — and much more reliable — message than her words. Her body language may be saying, "I'm not pleased with this" or "I'm not too sure about the way it's being presented" or "Speed it up, I'm ready to get out of here."

Employers can evaluate the messages their employees are sending to customers, clients or fellow workers and know whether that employee is hurting or helping business. And employees can learn to read the subtle signals a boss is sending in order to adjust their behavior accordingly.

In power-differential relationships, such as with superiors and subordinates, successful interactions depend on both parties being able to use and read body language. Superiors need to know how to make their subordinates comfortable while communicating their desires in order to get results. Subordinates need to know how to read the boss's subtle signals to discern the best way to approach professional situations. Between males and females in the workplace, correct use of body language can mean the difference be-tween friendliness and sexual harassment.

In my story, the manager was just a cave-dwelling hobbit. He didn't take in all the cues he could have. Once his work life was smoother and yours can be to. But it's not easy.

Our body language defines us

I was at an end-of-the-year event with my professional speaker associa-tion when a group of humorous speakers started doing impressions of other speakers. "Who's this?" one of them yelled. He bounded into the room and ran around a few times while wearing an exaggerated smile and yelled, "All right, okay, let's get started!" He dramatically pushed up his long sleeves to his elbows. Everyone laughed and pointed at me! Our body language defines us.

My parents used to play old records (yes, records on a turntable) of the comedians from the sixties who did impressions: Frank Gorshin, Rich Little, and John Byner. Their impressions of the top movie stars and celebs of the day like John Wayne and Edward R. Murrow were dead on. How did they do this? By studying the celebrities' body language and voice. The really good impressionists don't only imitate the broad strokes actors used in the movies, but also study and use those subtle movements and postures the celebrities use every day. The shake of a head, the darting of the eyes, or the glance worked into an impression made the impressionist into the person he or she was imitating. Good impressionists know nonverbal communication. And they know that body language defines you.

Have you ever watched Larry King on his nightly interview show? Does it seem like Larry shows more of an interest in his guests than other interviewers do? Here's why:

Larry started in radio and only switched over to TV relatively recently. Back in the old days there was only a tiny little table less than fourteen inches wide between the interviewer and the guest so they had to share a micro-phone. I still see them in some of the studios where I am interviewed. All those years interviewing guests in that intimate space has given Larry a great nonverbal interview style.

Larry leans in unusually close to his TV guests. This shows his interest in the guest. He has an unusual power that gives him the ability to get away with being that close. Add in his loud, bombastic voice, and you have an in-terviewer with great intensity. This intensity makes guests become intense dur-ing his interviews and makes his show fun to watch, which people have been doing since 1985.

Oprah has a way with her nonverbal communication we find enthralling. She can go from high energy, hands in the air, hips moving, pulling out all the stops when dancing with Tina Turner, to soft energy, using an almost blank face and emotionless voice with former criminals who are her guests, but her nonverbals always seem authentic. She has an unusually big smile and she laughs loudly. She has a way of turning her head and looking at her audience to make asides in a playful voice that creates intimacy with the television audience.

Bill Clinton is a master charismatic leader. He was one of the first presidents to come out from behind the podium when giving a speech! He has a small smile around the mouth, but a big crinkle around the eyes. His voice is warm and melodic. And here is the big one: For 10 years my audience members who have met him have described his hypnotic eye contact. "He looks right at you, so you feel like there is no else in the crowd," they all say. They all say the same thing, with none knowing what others have said. His body language defines him.

I am often asked by the media to read the body language of various bigwigs and celebs. The *New York Post* asked me to read the body language of "Today Show" host Katie Couric for one week, after rumors flew that there were problems on the show. I was to try to see if there were nonverbal signs saying she was unhappy, stressed or angry with the producer over contract disputes. Knowing Katie's ebullient personality, I knew any little ticks would be telling. She was as perky as ever, so I think things were fine. Perhaps she's just a true professional.

CNN had me on after the Katrina disaster to read President Bush's body language during the crisis. The public had noticed he was not his usual smiling self; he was sour faced, blinking and nervous in a interview with Matt Lauer, and his voice was downright angry and defensive as he talked about his choice for the U.S. Supreme Court. Our body language defines us, so any changes in our nonverbals are telling.

Body language improves our relationships

Back in college, I had a boyfriend who was gorgeous and very funny. When he walked down the street, his dark-haired Italian good looks would literally make women stop in their tracks to look, but when he opened his mouth, his funny, comic voice would surprise the girls that stopped to talk. He hated that surprised look on their faces. So he would act goofy to deal with it. After I had been dating this cutie for a while, I noticed he would become funny in response to anything negative he experienced and it began to irritate me. I didn't know what his true feelings were. I talked to him about it, but he made jokes when I brought it up. Some of his body language seemed depressed, but his words and playfulness were a mismatch. The inconsistencies wore on me. I wanted to see the real guy, and we eventually broke up. But we stayed friends even after he graduated and moved away. Two years later, he committed suicide.

Why do I share this very tragic story with you? Because his nonverbals were sending a loud and clear message that he was sad, but I didn't hear how desperate the message was. I didn't have all the information about body language to know how honest and true the nonverbals were. And most importantly, I didn't take significant action on my intuition. I lost a dear friend and the world lost a wonderful guy. I wish I knew then what I know now.

Knowing and understanding body language and using its secrets is valuable in your personal relationships in good times and bad, whether those relationships are intimate or just friendly. This nonverbal communication knowledge will help you build relationships that are happier and healthier, get others to like and love you, enhance your self-esteem, find out if your friends and family members are being honest, show your interest, respect, and love, and most importantly, to understand what your loved ones' needs are and to meet those needs.

It Makes us Feel Safer

When you were a child, your parents told you never to talk to strangers. As an adult, you don't have much choice. You are constantly encountering people you have never met before and may never see again. Can you trust the woman who is trying to sell you a used car? What about the man walking toward you on a deserted street?

One of my first workshops was for law enforcement personnel to learn how to identify duplicitous and deceitful behavior, and distinguish between ordinary nervousness and intentional deception. Of course, based on their years of experience, there were participants who were reading body language correctly, but by learning all the possible cues and understanding the science underlying their instincts, they learned to trust their hunches more. They learned to watch for a multitude of cues, and then I showed them how to analyze the context and read the cues in the correct order. You will learn the LOADED method that helps you do that in Chapter 3.

In today's stressful times, it's not just law enforcement and security personnel who need to know how to read body language. Anyone can be at risk from random acts of violence.

In the 1970's, I was in my sophomore year of college at Florida State. I lived in a beautiful dormitory, Gilchrist Hall, built in the 1900s on the old side of campus, right across the street from Sorority Row. It was an innocent time. The scariest thing we ever had to deal with was the faint possibility we might run into a streaker from the guys' dorm on a Saturday night. We felt safe. In one horrible evening that changed.

The girls in my dorm woke to find out that some of the girls in the Chi Omega house across the street from us, just 100 yards from our dorm, had been horribly brutalized and two of them had been killed. The attacker had also hurt girls in a house further down the street. The details were gruesome. A description of the attacker went out. The description described him as 5'8", slender, with dark brown hair and boyish looks. Posters of his police sketched face were put up all over campus.

I remember how the mood of the entire campus went from Florida beach sunny to gulf storm gray. People who had walked across campus the day before laughing, smiling and waving, who had flirted with strangers in the quad and given hugs to classmates, now had very different body language. The girls' body language had become tense. We walked in clusters, never alone, and we studied the faces of every man that approached us. If he looked anything like the broadcast description, we skirted away from him. In class, we left seats between ourselves and the men we did not know that well. We stopped going out at night. Fear honed our body language skills

The boys changed too. They walked with their heads bowed and avoided making eye contact. They walked slowly, giving us time to check them out. They sat grimly in the classrooms, fearful and ashamed they were men. It was as if they were sorry to make us feel so afraid just by coming close to us. Guy friends talked about how uncomfortable they all felt. Men I knew who matched the description at all avoided walking alone or at night. Fear changed the way they held their bodies. These changes were not just for a day but lasted for weeks. It persisted long after Ted Bundy, the attacker, was caught, long enough for this profound and terrible fear to bore deeply into us and steal our innocence.

Does that mean we have to mistrust every person with whom we come into contact? That fear should motivate us to change? Not at all. We can utilize the skills of a professional to evaluate quickly whether or not to open up and smile or to turn around and leave.

What is YOUR body saying?

Of course, all the concepts of body language and nonverbal communication apply not only to your customers, clients, peers, employees and loved ones, but also to you. Observation of others' body language cues is important, but you also need to observe the cues you are sending out. Truly knowing yourself creates confidence. No matter how well supported and prepared your words are, it is your nonverbal delivery that will establish your credibility. Self-examination is the key. As you continue through this book, you'll find more exercises to help you get a good idea of who you are and how you appear to the world.

Are you using the 7 secret features of body language?

Below are seven secret features of nonverbal communication, exercises to see how well you're using them and tips to improve your ability.

1. Nonverbal communication is ambiguous. You have to look at the whole package. You cannot look at just one aspect. When you're reading nonverbal communication, you have to read the whole body and the voice.

    Your boss comes into your office, head forward, a grimace on his face and his hands in tight fists. He comes up to you, throws his hands in the air, and growls out, "It's going to be a great day today!" But you know you are not going to have a great day.

    A young woman is at the end of a date. She turns to her date and says, "I had a great time" with a small smile as she quickly turns her back and scoots in the door. This leaves her date wondering, "Did she have a great time or not?" Since she did avoid the goodnight kiss, the answer is "probably not." She gave a purposefully ambiguous message. In girl talk, that means, "I don't want to be mean, but don't call again. "

    Tip: Have you given out an ambiguous message recently? Did you intend to? Were you trying to be nice? Funny? Or was there another motivation? What would have happened if you had been "straight" in your communication? The next time you catch yourself sending an ambiguous message, freeze-frame and ask yourself, "Would this relationship improve if I gave an honest matching response"?

2. Nonverbal communication is continuous. It doesn't stop even if you want it to, so you have to keep on reading it.

    I was over at a friend's house on a Sunday afternoon for a get-together planned weeks in advance. I was welcomed warmly into the house with a tender hug and a smile and then led out to the deck where two guy friends were sitting. Then the host asked me if I wanted some iced tea and went to get me a drink. I read that she was happy to see me and I looked forward to a nice day. When the host returned, she silently set the glass in front of me and sat in a chair far away. She didn't join in our conversation but instead would occasionally take a deep breath and try to hold it until it would sort of fizzle out. Several times, she looked toward the house and pressed her hand to her head. It took me a good five minutes to realize that I couldn't go by the first few signals that told me the host was in a good mood.

Her secret signals continued after her nice obligatory first-impression greeting. The signals of space and silence said that she was somewhere else. The touch to the forehead and her looking at the house indicated that something was on her mind. Holding her breath communicated that she was trying to stuff it.

I asked a few casual questions and found out that our host was overwhelmed at work from a crisis on a big project. She had worked all weekend and had more work to do. I realized she didn't want or need company all afternoon and suggested we change our plans to a shorter visit. Immediately, all was right with the world. The host said she never would have "said" anything, but would have stayed up all night working.

Or imagine this: At your company's annual meeting in Palm Beach, the head honcho is telling your team what's happening for the next quarter. She is talking in a clipped and angry voice and she is not smiling. You want to be outside playing golf, or lounging by the pool catching some rays, but if you want to save your department's budget, you have to understand everything she says. You have to get the real skinny: every nuance of what she feels and what she thinks. You cannot miss a blink or a word. She keeps on talking, her voice changes, is lighter and happy, her head nods up and down as she talks about the next quarter. You are taking notes furiously. You wish she would slow down, but her body language keeps on going and going, farther than a bunny on Energizer batteries and a triple espresso. You have to keep reading the signals and note when the changes occur.

3. Nonverbal communication is multi-channeled. Unlike when we use words, we can use all five senses to enrich the messages we send and decipher the messages we receive.

    You read the email and it says "the training will cost $20,000" but when you are in the room with the research team leader and she says those words, you can watch her face and body language, hear her voice and know whether she thinks it is a great price, a reasonable price, or a ridiculously high price.

Tip: Make it a habit NOT to send emotional messages via email. Email was designed to send academic information and in today's world, you should ideally only use it to send facts. The receiver of an emotional email can't see your body language and your words. They do not have the full message and you can get into trouble.

4. Nonverbal communication is emotionally revealing. The words on the page, "I am really angry at you" mean very little to us. We need the nonverbal actions to paint the picture and to make us feel what the other person feels. I was listening to a speaker give a bi-annual report that would affect his budget and project for the coming year. He turned toward the screen to read a slide filled with data and with no expression on his face (or what little I could see of the side that was visible). He read in a flat monotone voice, "The gains with this proposed change will save the company $3 million." He then went on to read the rest of the slide. The committee did not respond to that startling statistic. They did not give a darn. And months later when I was asked back to give speech coaching to the group I found that the speaker had not gotten his proposed cost increase. He didn't know that reading makes your voice go monotone and ironically, he hadn't thought it appropriate to get excited by the numbers!

Tip: You need to communicate the emotion you want your audience to feel. If your child is describing meeting Mickey Mouse for the first time, the neon smile on his face, the excited gestures, and his gleeful voice will transport you to that moment with him.

Exercise

To help you understand how nonverbal behavior and body language affect the way you communicate with others, I will be asking you to take part in various exercises as you read this book. In our first exercise, try this:

Stand or sit in front of a mirror and say the lines below in at least four different ways. Make sure you change your voice and give full facial expressions and gestures. For example, say it sarcastically out of the side of your mouth with an eye roll; with energy, a smile and a raised arm; with conviction, an open mouth and pounding fist; in a defeated whisper with a sad expression and hands behind your back, and so on. Notice how the meaning changes depending on your vocal delivery and your facial expressions and gestures.

- "I'm so sorry."
- "It's no big deal."

- "You did it."
- "No."
- "Please, let's forget all about it."
- "Whatever you want is fine with me."
- "The deadline is Sept 26th."

Did you notice a difference? Did you see how you communicate your message with more than your words? The true meaning of a message comes from the timing, the situation or environment, the facial expression, gestures, posture, space and voice — not the words.

Many times people use the right positive words with a negative delivery and hide behind the words. How many of you have heard this one, but the body language didn't match the words?

"But I said I loved you."

In the short run, you can get away with hiding behind the words you say, but if you are often sending contradictory messages where your words and nonverbal cues don't match, people will stop feeling safe around you. They will think you lack integrity and just plain won't trust you.

5. Nonverbal communication is more believable. Voltaire put it best — "One great use of words is to hide our thoughts." Our physical actions show whether the words belie our true intentions. For instance, you and a co-worker were up for the same promotion, but he gets it. As you're walking down an office corridor later on that day, you see him coming the other way. You know you can't avoid him, so you prepare for the meeting in the middle of the hall. You put out your hand and say, "Congratulations," with a smile. But your neck and shoulders have stiffened and he can feel the tension in your hand. And as in our earlier "no kiss date" example, the words were not as true as the nonverbals."

6. Nonverbal communication is more culturally specific. From culture to culture, body language meaning changes more than the meanings of word do. However, specialists say children are born with an inherent body language that is common to all peoples. They learn different, specific actions as they develop. When you go to Paris and talk loud on the Metro, the very volume of your voice communicates to a Frenchman that you are rude.

7. Nonverbal communication uses a different part of our brain. Our brains process nonverbal communication differently than they process words.

According to Peter Russell in *The Brain Book*, "The brain can receive the visual image of a person's face in a hundredth of a second; analyze its many details in a quarter of a second; and synthesize all the information into a single whole, create a full-color experience of the face, recognize this face out of thousands of others recorded in memory, and recall details about the person as well as associations and ideas connected with the person, all in less than a second. At the same time it will be interpreting the expression on the face...generating emotional feelings toward the person...and deciding on a course of action...and adjusting the body."

Obviously then, nonverbal communication gives us different information than a person's words do, and the information is processed in different parts of the brain. The left hemisphere of the brain controls our language faculties (except for profanity!), and our analytical and reasoning capabilities. The left-brain sees the details but it cannot see the whole. It can see the nose, the lips, the eyes, but it cannot see a face. The right brain can visualize, comprehend and perceive a complex set of cues and make it into a whole. It takes the nonverbal cues and infers their meaning, based on only a few features because of its ability to fill in the blanks. This is where spatial, pictorial, gestalt (the big picture), and emotional reactions seem to be centered. The right brain is therefore more adept than the left in reading emotional facial expressions and in determining mood and emotional states by reading a person's voice and body language. It is even more sensitive to the emotional nuances conveyed by touch. The right brain also memorizes and recalls emotional experiences.

Chapter 2

How Do You Look to Others: The Messages You Send

REMEMBER THE MANAGER WHO ACTED LIKE A HOBBIT? HE HAD NO idea how other people saw him.

At work, we are often unaware how the most mundane nonverbal behaviors affect the way everybody views us. We can walk around as clueless and foolish about our nonverbal blind spots as someone with spinach between their teeth. As I share this story, take note of the nonverbal behaviors and your perception.

Fresh out of graduate school and very young and naïve, I went to work for a company. After working in academia, I already had a successful consulting firm. I brought my clients with me and soon had new ones. A percentage of each of the contracts I produced went to the firm. The office had no hours or procedures to keep. You came when you wanted to, did what you wanted to do and left whenever. I was on the road almost every week and got back in late at night so I rarely got to the office before 10:00 am. I would say hello, visit with the support staff near the door and then go immediately to my corner office.

Back then, I dressed to the nines to speak, always wore pantyhose and high heels and spent an hour on my waist-length hair. But after a week of that, I began to go into work casually dressed, long before casual dress became the norm in offices. I wore pants and comfortable shoes, and I left my hair natural rather than curled. I worked until 4:00 and took a lunch break. I did not accept offers to lunch with fellow workers or visit with them in their office. I was too busy working.

The entire building cleared out at 5:00 on the dot. I usually stayed until 8:00 or 9:00 and then Mac the security guy kindly escorted me from the building. The company was going through some hard times, so I took more jobs than I personally needed to take and traveled a heck of a lot more than any sane person should. I worked so much that I had no life other than work, but as far as I knew, I was the only person bringing cash flow to the company. I didn't bring much, but a little was more than nothing was.

Yet, I was puzzled. None of my coworkers had ever brought me in on their long-term projects. One day, I was in the office making sales calls, which was always fun. I knew my clients well and I would spend sales days laughing and visiting on the phone. Oddly, a new employee specializing in sales kept going back and forth in front of my office. I would signal, but he didn't want to talk. Nearing 4:00, I gathered up the notes from all the contracts I had booked and carried them down to my assistant (This was long before we had computers on our desks or such a radical thing as email). Then I went to the break room where the new guy found me sitting on my feet and munching on a fajita salad.

"Hey. I heard you making all those personal calls today on the company long distance line. You were having so much fun. You were laughing all day," he said.

I thought I had heard wrong and said, "Excuse me?"

"I am not going to tell anyone you were making personal calls all day, I just wanted to rib you because you were so much fun to watch."

I was shocked and managed to garble out, "No, I was making sales calls today."

"Sure you were," he joked, "So was I."

"No, I was really making sales calls. I just took notes for four contracts down to get typed and mailed out."

Now it was his turn to be surprised. He paused quite awhile and then said, "That's how you make sales calls?" Suddenly, my professional career flashed before my eyes. To this sales trainer and to everyone in the office, I was the little blonde who came in late and laughed on the phone! No wonder they did not see me as a professional. By the nonverbal behaviors they could see, I wasn't. It turns out nobody but the office manager knew I was bringing in money; they stopped sharing profit information in Friday morning meetings I missed because I was late! I had messed up royally! I was teaching nonverbal communication and forgot I was communicating every time I went into the office.

What no one will tell you

There is a makeover TV show called What Not to Wear. On the show, friends and family members appalled at how someone they know dresses, request the person get a makeover. I find the show entertaining on many levels. Why are the bad dressers always so surprised they were chosen for the show?

- The friends and family never told them
- Or, they didn't believe what they were told
- Or, they do not know what good dressing looks like

Think about it. Most of your friends and family are strangely uncomfortable telling you what's wrong with you (except perhaps your mother and your spouse, but that's a different book). They may make a face when you wear that too tight shirt but they won't say, "You cannot wear that anymore. You have gotten too fat!" And then if people do tell you, you ignore it. You think, "But it's my favorite shirt" or you think, "I have always looked good in this shirt. In fact, ever since junior high, I have looked hot in this!" Finally, you may not know what snappy dressing looks like. You need someone who will show and model good dressing.

On the show, the fashion consultants put the guest in a four-way mirror booth so they can see themselves from all sides. That alone is painful for the guest. Then they come in and start coaching. They are brutally honest. They say things like, "You look horrible in that." "That color is awful with your hair color." "These shoes went out in the 80's when they were never in." Then they give coaching on good dressing and even use mannequins dressed appropriately to show what the person should look like. Finally, they have the person go and shop for the clothes and wear them.

You may not be a bad dresser or have poor body language, but you might want to improve. There may be things you don't know about yourself. If you want to improve your body language, you need to get into a four-way mirror on your behavior, be brutally honest with yourself, find models of the best nonverbal behaviors and change your behavior.

What follows is the "How do I look" exercise that will help you do just that. I created the exercise for myself the day the sales guy talked to me in the break room. I needed something — a four-way, mirrored booth — to help me see where the gap was between how I saw myself nonverbally and how others saw me. I made a list of how I viewed myself, my behaviors that were viewable, and then what anyone viewing the behaviors would think of that person.

This has since become one of the single most important exercises in my workshops and coaching. It is one of the first things I did with the hobbit manager from the first chapter. It is an exercise that changed my life. I have been told many times over the years that it has helped others overcome their blind spots and to learn how others look at them. If you are someone who skips all the exercises in books, please take the time and do this one. It may blow you away.

Exercise
Try the following self-evaluation to see how you are coming across to others:

(a) Take out a sheet of paper and create three columns.

(b) In the first column, write your self-perception — all the things you believe to be true of you. If you work, first list all the things that you believe are true about the way you see yourself as an employee, supervisor, co-worker etc. My list in the story would have said professional workaholic, great speaker, team player and so on. Then make a list of how you see yourself in personal situations, say as a spouse, parent, and friend. The list should include personality characteristics, adjectives and adverbs you believe about you. Examples might include happy, strong, overbearing, calm, friendly, and shy.

(c) In the second column, write your nonverbal behaviors — all the things that others see you do. You must be honest with yourself here. My list included a messy desk, and sitting childlike on my feet at meetings (the few I did go to). For work, write everything that your team sees you do. Don't write down anything you do behind closed doors or that you tell others you do (or they should know you do), but only the things they actually see you doing. I couldn't write down that I got standing ovations and great critiques. Those things were invisible and irrelevant to them. This is critical. Typically, these are the things you do when you are interacting with them, face-to-face, on the phone or through email. List all of these items as nonverbal behaviors. They should be things a scientist looking down on you would write down in the lab book, not perceptions. For example, instead of writing down "friendly," you would write, "they see me come into work every day and say hello to everyone with a smile on my face and cheery voice." Instead of "businesslike," you would write, "They see me grumpy and hunched over until I have my coffee," or "They see me go directly to my computer and start working without stopping to smile or wave at anyone." The list of work behaviors could include

- How and when you come into work each day
- The way you usually dress from your shoes up to your head
- What your office/cube and desk looks like

- What your standard everyday nonverbal facial expressions and voice are like
- How often you work in your cubicle or where others can see you
- How you visit or do not visit others and what your nonverbal behavior is like when you do.
- How you respond to phone calls and emails: quickly, slowly, never
- How you answer your phone and how you talk on it
- How you respond to visits to your office/cubicle
- What your lunch behavior and break room behavior are like
- Where do you sit at meetings?
- What is your one on one and big meeting behavior? Do you listen, speak, and doodle?
- How quickly or slowly you respond to requests (time is a nonverbal communicator)
- How you treat different people
- How and when you leave work each day
- Whether you socialize after work and what you do

(d) Look at all those "seen" behaviors. In the third column, write others' perceptions of you — what you would say about another person you saw doing those things. That means, "What would people say about someone if those behaviors were all they could see?" This was also a revelation. No wonder I wasn't pulled in on projects! The other guys didn't even know who I was or what I could do. I was just a laughing, casually-dressed kid. What is your objective perception of those behaviors? You might even show just that column to other people and ask them what they would think of that person. Take it to your boss and see what he says. Sit down with your sweetie and see what he or she says. What do your kids see and what would they say?

(e) Now compare the first column with the third column. How does your perception of yourself compare with others' perceptions of you? Are you coming across the way you think you do? Are you coming across the way you want to?

(f) Finally, make a list of actions you are willing to change if you need to and behaviors you should continue. Set up meetings at work.

Exercise 11

There is another step to this process: Imagine yourself as the best person you can possibly be. It's important to have real life models of the characteristics you want. Then you can look at the people and see the behaviors to model.

Make a list below of all the people you admire. They can be people you have known personally, famous leaders, celebrities or fictional characters in movies and books. Three of the people on my list are Oprah Winfrey, Ted Clevenger (former dean of communication at FSU), and my friend Elaine. If you have trouble with this list, let it simmer on the back burner for a while. As you go to sleep at night during the next week, ask yourself to dream about people you admire and wish to emulate.

Now write a list of those admirable people's characteristics. Go to your list of admirable people and list the aspects of their personalities you admire. This is what my list looked like:

- Oprah — honesty, sincerity and sense of humor
- Ted Clevenger — honesty, sincerity, integrity, intelligence, the ability to read people, and compassion.
- My friend Elaine — honesty, intelligence, compassion, and warmth.

Be thorough.

Now start your behavior list.

Look at your list of characteristics and just as you did for that list, write down what each of these people do to show they have these characteristics. What is it about their voice, posture, gestures, use of time, eye contact and so on that you like and wish to emulate? Write every behavior on your behavior list. As you finish with that person, go on to the next and write their behaviors below the last person's. If any of the nonverbal behaviors repeat with a different person put a tick mark next to it.

Now you have a list of ideal behaviors. You know exactly where successfully doing those behaviors will lead. If you are practicing these behaviors, you will be one of the most admirable people you know.

WHY WE ARE LACKING BODY LANGUAGE SKILLS

I have a business acquaintance who works for a major broadcasting company. Her job is exciting, challenging and causes her to work 80 hours a week. She has conflicts with people at work, no deep friendships outside of work and barely has the strength to grocery shop or do her laundry on weekends. She told me, "I am not sure why I have all these problems, but I suspect it could be my body language and my inability to read people. "I know body language is important. I know I mess up and don't pick up on cues I should. Why am I having such a hard time?

She does not have the time, the strength, or the emotional resources to practice good body language interaction. There are many reasons we lack body language skills or not use them.

1. Time constraints. We are overworked and overstressed. We lack face-to-face time at work because there are so many tasks to accomplish. With family, it's a matter of keeping a good calendar, being a taxi service and outsourcing. We are too tired from work to be close to each other and it creates a cycle. The lack of practice communicating makes it hard and stressful to get close, so we may work more to escape family life. If we are single, we may work more to escape the scary prospect of the dating and romantic relationships.

   What you can do: If you're suffering from time constraints, you may want to budget time at work and home to communicate face to face. Liken it to scheduling time to work out to improve your physical health. Put it in your daily calendar, or computer calendar: I will spend fifteen minutes from 9:00 to 9:15 visiting with a coworker; I will take my boss to lunch this month; This week, I will join a book group or continuing ed class that meets each week and go no matter how tired I am; on Tuesday nights, I'll turn the TV off and have the family eat dinner in the dining room.

2. The desire to have everything happen quickly. Instant messaging and in-stant relationships give us little patience for the subtle nuances of the tim-bre of a voice or the subtle shoulder shrug.

   In 1967, Marshall McLuhan, the father of mass communication, said, "Any technology gradually creates a totally new human environment." With the advance of email, beepers, fax machines, the Internet and so forth, our technology has sped up the pace of our lives and has under-scored our need to understand others more quickly.

   Since we lead such busy lives, our interaction times with others are shorter. Today when we meet people, they have a couple of minutes to impress us before we move on. My mother said when she was growing up in a small town in Pennsylvania, you would see someone and per-haps only make eye contact for months before you said hello, and even more months would pass before you had a conversation. Not only did you have time to make an assessment slowly and carefully, you could ask everybody else in town about the person who interested you and get their opinions. You had the gift of time.

   Now we have "speed dating." Singles often go to a coffeehouse or a bar and sit with a potential partner for three minutes, make an assess-ment, and then a bell sounds — and they're off to the next table to meet someone new. (For those of you who haven't been on the dating scene lately, this really exists. Incredible. No pressure, right?)

What can you do? Take a day or a morning each week to give face-to-face the messages you would have sent by email.

3. Increase in technology. TV (#1), email, voicemail, PDA. We get sucked in with the quick message instead of the full message.

4. Loss of rituals that created body language modeling and practice. I had several favorite TV shows as a child. One was The Waltons, about a large extended family that lived together in one house. Another was Andy Griffith where they sat on the porch in the evening and talked to each other, and the guys got together at the barbershop. The children had all those models and guidance. Instead, today we put the old parents in nursing homes and sit in front of the tube rather than on the porch. Later I enjoyed The Odd Couple, where the guys would play poker with each other and visit. Some of my favorite family memories from childhood are from playing a card game called Michigan Rummy with the family on Friday nights. We would laugh, talk and eat popcorn. I loved family car trips where we would sit side by side for hours and hours. We would really listen to each other's voices and hear the subtle nuances. We honed our skills and became closer. Eight years ago, hungry for new rituals, I created a game group. We have been meeting for years to play spades, dominoes and poker. Sitting close together and face to face around the card table month after month has helped us learn thousands of subtle nonverbal cues, including how to read each other's poker "tells." We have also become much closer friends.

Exercise
List three rituals that you can add to your life to improve the quality of your interactions.

5. Lack of face-to-face time.
    I'm sure you will agree with me that there is less face-to-face communication than even ten years ago. We talk to our friends and family members on the cell phone, read messages on the pager and computer screen, and talk to each other in cars with our hearts and heads toward the road, rather than toward each other. What ever happened to looking into someone's eyes?
    Speaking of looking into someone's eyes, people don't even need to meet anymore to begin dating. In 2005, Match.com estimated it had matched 200,000 people through internet dating. And eHarmony.com

said that 10,000 people had gone to the altar after meeting on its site since its inception in 2000. Talk about lack of face time.

Business colleagues complain they don't get to meet potential clients. The customer goes to their website, clicks on a button that says "send me information" and then asks for pricing by email. Nobody gets to take the measure of the other person in this kind of business interaction.

Various reports say that parents now spend an average of only one hour a week in face-to-face contact with their children. That means one hour a week to pick up on cues that would let us know how our siblings, parents, spouses or children are doing. Just one hour to show them how you are doing. Even our familial interactions occur as sound bites: "Mom, I need my red shirt for the school dance ... Make sure you're not out late tonight ... I am so tired today."

With so little time together, and the time we do have so rushed, how do parents even know when there's a problem? Well, there are thousands of body language cues — a door shut loudly, a late arrival home, a love song that's played over and over on the stereo, a sigh, averted eyes, a meal partially eaten — that can help us understand and nurture our familial relationships. How many of us who grew up in the 60s and 70s wailed in the shower to the words of James Taylor's Fire and Rain? If our parents had been watching and listening to what was not being said, perhaps there wouldn't have been a generation gap!

An important ritual for learning nonverbal communication

I was sitting at the dinner table with my friends Bob and Renee and their daughters, six-year-old Morgan and two-year-old Madison. Bob raised his voice ever so slightly and said, "Morgan, it's not your turn to talk. Your mother was talking." Renee leaned over her two-year-old's high chair, touched the side of her head lovingly and said sternly, "Madison, don't talk with your mouth open. Finish chewing, then talk."

Bob and Renee then turned in their chairs and leaned forward toward Morgan, giving their full attention as Bob asked, "Tell us what you did in school today." Morgan's face broke into a smile as wide as a watermelon wedge and she began sharing the art project she did. Her parents' interest did not waver as they nodded their heads and kept asking her questions. They didn't even take a bite of food until Morgan threw up her hands and said, "That's all!"

Bob turned to me and asked where I had been traveling. I said "Florida." Little Morgan turned in her chair, made direct eye contact and asked loudly, "Did you go swimming a lot?" I answered no, marveling that a six-year-old knew how to ask follow-up questions.

As I sat there, I marveled at the constant, gentle corrections and sweet encouragements. I had noticed this each month when I had dinner with them, but this night I started counting the verbal and nonverbal coaching. I stopped when I got to 22 coaching statements or nonverbal corrections, such as a raised eyebrow of reproach, or a head nod of approval.

You may know about the research that shows a strong relationship between teen dropout rates and drug use and how many times a family eats dinner together. It seems like such a small thing, but one way to help teens stay in school, avoid drugs, and improve their interpersonal skills is by having family dinner together at least three times a week. Those parents who do obviously make use of that extra time to communicate verbally and nonverbally with their children. Here is what you may not know. We actually need to eat dinner with our families at least three times a week growing up to learn proper interpersonal communication and, most importantly, nonverbal communication.

Remember the story of the hobbit manager who sent emails to the guys in the adjoining cubicles? He didn't get the 18 years of modeling and coaching on nonverbal communication. He didn't learn the secret language of success. Sometimes, when we miss some subtle cue or bit of humor, we might say jokingly, "Well I must have missed that meeting." What if you missed all those important dinners? If you did, you need to pay more careful attention to body language.

Guess what else your dining habits do? They set a pattern for your relationships later in life. For example, I had two childhood dinner tables. Being the baby of the family by many years, as a small child I either ate in one of two places: by myself on a TV tray in the basement so my parents and more mature siblings could have a "quiet" meal, or in the middle seat where I would sing dance, play with my food and do amusing things to gain the attention of the adults and distract them from their boring conversation. Eventually, I became a quiet observer as well as a good comedian, so I was allowed to stay at the table! As an adult, I can clearly see a relationship between my nonverbal behaviors at dinner with my nonverbal behavior with groups.

Exercise

Draw a picture of your family dinner table growing up. Put your name by the seat where you ate and then write in the names of everyone else. If you ate in front of the TV, draw that. Now draw lines between who talked to whom the most. Finally, shut your eyes and imagine your body language, your voice at the dinner table, and then the body language of others.

- What were your nonverbal behaviors at the table?
- How did you feel at the family dinner table?
- How did others treat you?
- Where do you tend to sit at conference tables as adult?
- How do you act at meetings today?

Are there any similarities between your behavior as a child and your adult behaviors and relationships?

6. Increased anxiety. We lack body language skills, so our anxiety increases. Our anxiety increases, so we fear interactions, especially those that require impromptu discussions and small talk. In 2002, $60 million was spent to promote Paxil, an anti-anxiety pill. As of that year, 37 million Americans were using it.

   We don't take the time to learn how to read others and get feedback on whether our guesses at people's messages are accurate. We just put our heads down and hope everything comes out all right.

   What can you do? Do the exercises in this book and talk about what you are learning with the people in your life.

Chapter 3

How to Read Body Language

YEARS AGO, I WAS DATING A MAN WHO LIVED IN A BEAUTIFUL LITTLE house. Every night after work, I would drive across town to his place, knock on his door and he would throw open the door with a grin on his face and pick me up off the ground in a big bear hug. I loved this hug. It was the best part of my day. I so looked forward to it.

One day, he did not answer the door. I knocked again. He still didn't answer. I waited a minute and then rang the doorbell, still no answer. Then I checked the garage and rang the bell again. I heard him yell, "Come on in, the door's open." As I entered the house, I saw him at the dining room table, his face and upper body hidden behind an upraised Wall Street Journal. Only his legs were in view and turned towards me as I approached him. He did not otherwise acknowledge my presence. What do you think I was feeling? What worries do you think I had? I wondered what I had done wrong or what I had said. I rewound the tape of our most recent day together, analyzing every word said and every facial expression and got very upset. But before I blamed myself for possibly upsetting him or got on his case for his behavior, I took a deep breath.

As I breathed deeply, my obsessing stopped and I was able to think clearly. I realized I was reading the body language in the wrong order. I realized what may have caused his nonverbal cues was something going on inside of him, something that had nothing to do with me. So I sat down and talked to him through the paper.

I found out he been arguing on the phone with his teenage daughter. Right when I first knocked, she was telling him she was dropping out of school. They yelled at each other just as I knocked again. His daughter hung up on him. I knocked a third time. He was not mad at me, but rather upset with himself and his daughter. I was just the next person on the scene.

In this chapter you will learn the steps to reading body language. One of the most important is to interpret the cues you get correctly. What is the most likely thing to motivate someone's behavior? The most likely reason that a person does anything is what is going on with him. Don't assume you motivated the behavior.

BEWARE OF HASTY INTERPRETATIONS

You're in the company cafeteria when you spot Rita, a fellow employee whom you like and respect very much. When she spots you, she begins to walk the other way. You may think: "She doesn't like me anymore. There's a problem between us."

Making this conclusion may cause you to confront and argue with her, avoid her yourself, or have any number of other responses.

The problem with this kind of hasty interpretation is that the primary motivator of nonverbal cues is what's going on with someone personally at that particular moment. For example, Rita may be avoiding you because she may be having problems at home or may be having financial difficulties. She wants to avoid you because she doesn't want to find herself talking about those concerns.

The second motivation underlying someone's nonverbal behavior is the person's own sensitivity about the topic you are discussing, especially if it touches on a personal situation. A friend of mine was at a party where she was telling a small group of people a couple of stories about people in her neighborhood running the same oddly placed stop sign and the look on their faces when they realized it. My friend did not say this was good or bad and none of the stories made light of the seriousness of running the stop sign. In the middle of one of the stories, another woman gave her a pained look, abruptly turned her back on the conversation, and left the party. My stunned friend didn't know what she had said or done wrong and spent the rest of the night agonizing over whether she talked too loud or had looked too goofy telling her stories. She even called me to mull over what detail of her behavior could have caused someone to "not like her." She later learned the woman had been involved in a car accident with someone who ran a stop sign. It wasn't my friend's voice or gestures that had caused the reaction. Bringing up the topic had set the woman off more than anything my friend did nonverbally.

Most interestingly, the least likely reason for someone to send cues is their response to the person with whom they are interacting. In other words, it's usually nothing personal. So, if you receive signals from someone — say lack of eye contact or turning away — your ideal first response should be, "I wonder what's going on with him that makes him so uncomfortable? I wonder if it was the topic. Is it that we started discussing money? I wonder if it was the situation. Is it that we are sitting in my office?" Finally, you might ask yourself, "Is it me? Do I have bad breath?" More often than not, it has nothing to do with you.

Don't take one body language cue and decide you "know" what another person is trying to communicate. You must read the whole person. Although we can give various interpretations for various nonverbal signals, it is important to keep in mind that we must check each of these signals before drawing any conclusions.

So, let's recap.

The most important motivators of body language, in order of their significance:

- What's going on inside us most profoundly affects our shifts and changes in body language. For example, if we are tense, happy, or having a good day, our body language will shift to match our emotional state. If we are talking to someone, he or she may yawn and rub their eyes not because we are as boring as a meeting on the annual report, but because they are tired!

- The topic or situation being discussed is the next likely motivator of our body language. For example, your body might be animated when talking about baseball, and tense when talking about money. Or if you are talking to someone, he might smile and be comfortable when you talk about dogs, but get irritated when you talk about the IRS.

- The people we are with can motivate us to change or shift our body language. We might relax, sit back and prop our feet up when friends come over, but sit on the edge of the couch with our backs like sticks when it's a visit from the minister. When we are talking to someone else, they may turn away from us, break eye contact or lean forward, depending on whether they hate us or love us to pieces.

Missing Cues

I was sitting in a restaurant with my friend Ann when her friend Deb came up and started talking to us. Sitting with a laptop between us, and papers stacked everywhere; we told Deb we were meeting over lunch for a marketing session. But Deb kept talking, leaning over our table and going a mile a minute. Ann and I each made a brief response to Deb, "That's nice" from me and "That's interesting" from Ann. After that, Ann sat stiffly in her chair, feet turned away from Deb and towards me as she crossed her arms and looked down at her laptop. She did not give one verbal "uh-huh" utterance to encourage Deb to keep talking. I too remained tense and mute and flipped through the papers in front of me.

With my chest and torso turned towards Ann and not the chatty Deb, minutes ticked by. Oblivious to these cues, Deb kept right on talking. Ann bit her lip, stopped making any eye contact with Deb and looked around the restaurant, hoping the waiter would interrupt Deb. Ann's face finally gave an expression of anger, making her lip flatten out. Deb kept right on talking.

Ann and I were trying to be nice. Like many women, we were trying to be subtle and use our body language to send Deb the message that we were not interested in what she was saying. We sent cue after cue, but Deb was not getting the message. Finally, I said very gently, "Deb, could you forgive us? Ann and I are short on time for our meeting. We would love to visit more, but we are on a deadline. I'm sorry." Deb said, "Oh, I had no idea you guys were busy" and we said our goodbyes.

Sometimes people do not pick up on subtle cues. We think we are screaming with our body language, but they don't hear.

What was going on there? Both Ann and I were giving numerous signals nonverbally. Deb was too busy talking to notice the subtle cues. She just noticed that we had not gotten up to leave while she was talking! While we could take one cue and make a conclusion about what was happening, looking at everything would have more than likely given us a totally different picture. Deb needed to use the LOADED method.

> **Tip:** *Ambiguity such as saying one thing verbally and something else nonverbally does not send a clear message. If you do that, do not get mad when the other person does not get the hidden message.*

> **Tip:** *As a gender, women are more likely to send ambiguous messages. So beware of the messages you send if you are a women and if you're a man receiving a mixed message, ask verbally for clarity.*

The LOADED method of reading body language

Have you every been in a lunch line and seen a tray full of different plastic wrapped sandwiches, picked one up and wondered what kind it was? Is it turkey with Swiss? Roast beef with mayo? Ham with mustard? Reading and analyzing someone's body language by looking at all the things they are doing is like taking apart a big sandwich to see what kind it is.

One of the things that makes nonverbal communication so different from spoken language is that most body language meanings are not understood from one isolated cue, such as a smile or a tilted head. Nonverbal cues can have many different meanings. When we are interacting, many cues are occurring at the same time.

To read body language with accuracy in situations such as this, I have created a six-step process called the LOADED method, as in "loaded" with meaning. Here are the steps:

1. Listen to the words: Do the words match or contradict the body language and paralanguage (nuances of the voice) message. What is or is not being said verbally

2. Observe the behaviors and their frequency. Exactly what nonverbal behavior do you observe and how often do the behaviors occur?

3. Analyze the timing: What is done and said before and after the cue or cues.

4. Distinguish based on the location on the body: Where does each of those behaviors occur on the body?

5. Examine the context: Look at the situation, the topic and the relationship between the people.

6. Determine characteristics by degree: Where do the behaviors fit on a scale or continuum of such behavior?

To understand nonverbal language, you may have to look at multiple behaviors occurring at the same time just as if you were looking at all the layers of a sandwich. Simply looking at the lettuce does not tell you what kind of sandwich you've got. And simply looking at one body language cue does not always tell you what someone is saying nonverbally.

The LOADED Method

Listen to the words to see if the words and nonverbal cues match. Listen for the message in silence.

The L in the LOADED method stands for Listen. The first thing you need to do when reading body language is to listen to the words the person is saying. Note inconsistencies when words and body or voice do not match

Earlier in the book, I talked about the wife who said, "Nothing's wrong" as she frowned, folded her arms and turned away from her husband. If you were her husband, you would pay more attention to her turning away than you would her words. When there is a lack of congruence between the non-verbals and the words spoken, we generally believe the nonverbal communication.

Examples of Contradictory messages.

- You ask a friend to give you a lift because your car is in the shop and she grimaces and says, "Sure."
- You ask someone for their help in a store. They say, "My pleasure ma'am, I will be right with you" and walk toward you as slow as molasses with a look that says "You put me out."
- You ask your coworker if he can get his part of the report to you right away and he says "No problem" while sighing heavily, looking at his watch and then rubbing his head as if it hurts.

Analyze: Do you accept the word messages that people give you and avoid any discomfort that might come from getting to the real message sent by their nonverbal behavior? Describe a time when you did this and what the results of ignoring a contradictory message were.

Tip: When someone's words contradict their message, ask yourself why they might be concealing the truth. Motivations for giving contradictory messages: lack of confidence; fear of not being liked; playing the role of their job title; concern for retribution for speaking the truth; not in touch with their real feelings; don't want to admit they are angry; desire to be considered nice.

Analyze: Have you ever given a contradictory message? Describe what happened. What did you say and what did you do and what was your motivation?

Tip: One of the things that will make you a better communicator is to notice when your own nonverbal messages are incongruent. If you say "I really love you," but you've turned away and your eyes are on the TV screen, you are incongruent. If you grimace and break eye contact while you're telling your boss you really want that project with Bob, your boss may see your true feelings.

Analyze

Now let's apply the Listen to the words step to one of the examples from this chapter. In the restaurant example, Ann's and my words were, "That's nice" but the lack of expression in our voices and our turning away said, "That's not that nice." Deb listened to the words but missed the contradictory cues.

The next insight you get from listening is the message you get from their absence. Silence communicates. If there are no words when there normally should be, pay attention. At first, Ann and I were making comments about what Deb shared. Then we sent a silence message that we were done listening. Deb heard the word message but missed that silence message.

In the first example, with my boyfriend in the beautiful house, he was not saying anything! There were no words. It would have been normal for him to immediately begin talking with me. I knew that silence meant there was a problem, so I searched for more information to tell me exactly what the silence meant. Notice that the absence of words is a nonverbal cue. When you notice it, don't assume you know what silence means. Keep loading on cues.

The next two steps in the LOADED method make sense to examine at the same time.

- Observe the Behaviors and Their Frequency. Exactly what nonverbal behaviors do you observe and how often do the behaviors occur?
- Analyze the timing. What is done and said before and after the cue or cues. What else is going on?

There is an exercise and check sheet at the end of this chapter to help you learn how to observe the behaviors and monitor the timing. In the boyfriend example, my first cue was that he did not come to the door when I knocked. That cue of absence was repeated several times. Repetition of a cue strengthens the cue's message. The next cues were paralanguage cues. He shouted in a loud, strident, angry voice, "Come on in. The door's open." The next set of cues was centered on this behavior at the table: he remained seated and hid himself behind the paper. In the final set of cues, his torso and feet turned toward me as I entered the room. The timing of the foot movement was telling. I knew that that cue was directly in response to me entering the room. The rest of the cues could have been motivated by something else. As we learned they were motivated by the phone conversation from his daughter.

Distinguish based on the location on the body

The fourth step in the LOADED method is to Distinguish based on the location. Where does each of those behaviors occur on the body?

When reading body language, our natural tendency is to focus on the person's face. But when you feel the need to turn on your super powers, you have to look at the whole body. I have mentioned before that the cues on the face are under the most conscious control. So people can lie to you or fake how they feel or even think they are feeling one way, but the lower portion of the body, especially that part from the waist down, will often tell you the truth. The messages sent by the torso and the feet tend to be the most honest so give them more credence. When you're observing someone, look low and pay attention to the cues from the waist down.

Let's go to our examples.

My boyfriend's upper body was hidden behind the newspaper; making looking at the lower body cues a no-brainer option. However, as I came towards him, his lower body and his feet turned toward me. If I hadn't gotten the idea his negative cues were not about me before, the torso and feet toward me would have said to me he was not mad or not very mad at me. Turning toward me that way signaled he was open to talk to me. This was such a good clear message. But many people would miss it or not give those cues the power they should

The other thing you need to do when looking at the location on the body is see if the whole body is sending a similar message. That's called body congruence. We talked about word and nonverbal congruence under "listen to the words." Now, we are looking for congruence in all the cues someone's body is giving. My boyfriend's face and upper torso were saying he wasn't interested in me, but his lower torso and legs disagreed. There was body incongruence. Deb and I may were giving an incongruent message when we said "That's nice." We may have initially given body cues that we were listening, but soon our whole bodies were sending cues that we were no longer interested in listening.

Nonverbal cues usually occur in what is called a "gesture cluster" — a group of movements, postures and gestures that should have roughly the same meaning or add up to the same meaning. The cues in a cluster are like words in a sentence. Just as it would be difficult to take the word "love" out of a sentence and know what the person means, it would be difficult to know exactly what crossed arms mean without looking at other body language cues. We saw this in the story of my friend Steve.

This is what we call "congruence" in body language. Don't assume too much from a single body language cue. Rarely does a single cue, in and of itself, indicate anything. People give out thousands of cues in less than a minute. When you see someone cross his or her arms and you say to yourself, "That person is feeling defensive," you are disregarding the rest of their body language sentence. Just as one word cannot be taken in isolation from a sentence and still communicate a whole message, one cue taken in isolation from all the other ones can rarely give you an accurate reading of the person. We can learn, however, which cues are more potent than others are and which ones need to be read first. You will learn, for example, that if the person crossing her arms also turns her legs away from you and grimaces when you mention price, it's the price that's making her unhappy.

I was out with friends when one of my friends saw an old boyfriend. She got very excited, called him over and introduced him to me. He shook my hand warmly and smiled, but at the same time looked over my shoulder and nodded to someone else. Though his body was turned toward me, His feet were turned away and he never fully met my gaze. There was no body congruence.

Examine the context

The next step in the LOADED method is to Examine the Context. Look at the situation, the topic and what's going on with both you and the other person. This is a little more complicated, but it is important, so I am going to explain it in detail and give you plenty of examples.

When I was reading the cues from my boyfriend, I assumed that the negative messages were motivated by something I had done. You learned at the beginning of this book that this isn't the likely motivation. We had dinner together all the time and this hadn't happened before! The relationship was going well, so it was pretty much a slam-dunk that something going on with him was causing the problem.

In the second example, Deb needed to pick up on our cues and notice that we had changed from welcoming and warm to closed as she continued to talk. The shift in our cues would have been a big hint to Deb that she caused the negative cues by continuing to talk past the normal quick visit time. If something happens when you enter the room, it may be you who motivated the change.

Determine characteristics by degree

Finally, we take the last step: Determine characteristics by degree. How intense are the cues? Where do the behaviors fit on a scale or continuum of such behavior?

Whenever you are analyzing body language, you will notice that everyone's behavior can be placed somewhere on a scale. Just as you would read the number of degrees on a temperature scale or the number of meters on a test tube, you can read body language on a scale from low to high (or warm to cold) on a particular trait or aspect. For instance, when you hear a friend's "hello" on the phone and gauge from the loudness to softness and strength to weakness your friend's mood, you have used placement continuums to read your friend's vocal "paralanguage."

There are dozens of body language "cues" and corresponding scales. For instance, the distance between two people is an indication of the feelings and relationship between them. The closer you are physically and the closer you generally are emotionally, the higher others can read your emotional closeness on the nonverbal scale of physical closeness. You can also read a person's "body windows" — eyes, shoulders and arms, legs and feet — on a scale from open when we are comfortable, to closed when we are not. In addition, we can observe differences in gender and power level less on a scale from submissive to dominant. Finally, we can read body honesty characteristics on a scale of credibility to deceit.

Exercise 1

Body Language Check List

When I do video body language interpretations for law enforcement and the media, I use a rather elaborate check sheet and go through the video frame by frame. You do not have to do that! But to get you started in creating a habit of looking for all the cues, try using this check sheet to read the body language of a few guests on your favorite talk show.

Write down behaviors in the first column and then if you can, record what they said when they did it. If no words occurred but something changed in the overall picture (like a new guest sitting down), write down what changed. If something shows up again, like the first guest scratching his or her nose, make a slash in the number of times column. Of course, some people have little habits, like clearing their throat that they do all the time with everybody, but it still means something. Let me repeat, do not ignore repeated cues.

		# of times	What were they saying?
1.	THE BODY OVERALL		
2.	EYES		
	a. pupil dilation		
	b. gaze		
	c. blinking		
3.	MOUTH		
	a. smiling		
	b. tongue movement		
4.	REST OF THE FACE		
5.	HEAD		
6.	HANDS OR GESTURES		

	# of times	What were they saying?
7. **TORSO**		
a. shoulders _____		
b. posture _____		
c. lean _____		
8. ADAPTORS (USE OF OBJECTS) _____		
9. FEET AND LEGS _____		

Exercise 11

Observe two different interviews on television — one that is friendly and one that isn't. Jot down the body language cues. How does the context enable you to interpret the same cues differently?

Consider these factors before interpreting

You may be asking, "Do I have to consciously pay attention to all this stuff?" You may think, "If I focus that hard all the time, I would never really be in the moment with anybody." Here's the good news: You do not have to use your full super-nonverbal reading powers all the time.

People often ask me if I get tired of reading body language all the time. I respond that I don't read body language all the time. I would have to be like Superman walking around in tights all day. Subconsciously, you bet I read them. And because so much of the reading is easy after learning these steps, certain things pop out at me the way Superman notices a fleeing criminal, a dentist sees bonded teeth or a plastic surgeon spots a facelift. But I do not use my fully conscious "super powers" all the time. Subconsciously or consciously I ask myself the four following questions before I rev up my super powers.

Does any thing seem unusual, odd or abnormal?

Whether I am looking at a photo of Jennifer Anniston or a video of the president the first thing I look for are things that do not seem right. Is there anything I am looking at that doesn't fit or that does not seem normal? It's part of our gut first impression. When we are reading body language, contrasts stand out. For instance, if someone says one thing but the actions say something else, that is an important contrast. In fact our emotions will intensify if we see something unusual. Noticing big differences is part of our survival instincts. It's very important to notice the big contrasts.

Several years ago, a participant from one of my programs was flying to California from the East Coast with his girlfriend. His girlfriend nudged him and with a high and tight whisper said, "Watch these four guys in front of us. They look weird." She pointed to four gentlemen. The first one was sitting one row in front and across from them on the aisle. Another was a few rows in front of him and two others were on the same side of the plane as my participant, separated by several rows.

The man just to their left had his head down and his hands on his lap. Watching the hands, my participant noticed they would occasionally lift up and tighten into partial fists. The man was also sweating profusely. Also, he would lift his eyes and make contact with the three men in front of him, all without lifting his head.

Each of the three men glanced back furtively at what seemed like timed intervals. Their eyes were never met with a smile; at most, there was a slight bob of the head. None of the men talked with each other over the seats or got up, talked and visited with one another as you would normally do if you were traveling together. They obviously were of the same nationality and knew one another. None of the other men was carrying any bags or was reading or talking to anyone near them. All four men just sat. Their behavior did not seem normal.

My participant Jim became as disturbed as his girlfriend was. He went back and surreptitiously told the stewardess, who told him not to worry. When they all got off the plane, my participant's girlfriend was still so disturbed by the men that she insisted they report them to security. They took the time to give security a clear description. She had even written down their seat numbers inside a novel she had been reading.

Weeks passed. On September 11th, 2001, the fellow from my workshop and his girlfriend were watching the news and saw faces of the four men they had seen on their plane to Los Angeles — they were the four terrorists on one on the planes that hit the towers. The FBI called them soon afterwards and confirmed their story. Interestingly, the FBI said that several other people on my participant's flight had called after the flight to report the suspicious behavior.

Why did the FBI not research the men after the initial report and perhaps prevent the September 11th tragedy? The answer is they didn't see the behavior as abnormal. Seeing four nervous men on a plane did not seem the least bit abnormal. The participant and his girlfriend were in a confined space and noticed the body language was not normal, but the flight attendant and security did not see it that way. Prior to 9/11, they had no context of four airplane-riding terrorists to make them think four unusually nervous men, who are traveling together but not sitting together is not normal.

I am a frequent flyer, and so I usually board the plane early. For 10 years, I would sit in the airport, board the plane and notice the people getting on. It was a game of people watching. But since the tragedy of 9/11, I look at people very carefully, and it's no longer a game. I look for behaviors that are not normal. The context has changed.

What's going on with you?

The next thing to consider before revving up your super powers. Is what is going on with you. What's going on in your head? What's been happening in your life? For example, if you are having a really stressful day, you might be pretty oblivious to other people's subtle cues. That is actually a good time to rev up your super powers and read the body language correctly. Otherwise, you could misinterpret these cues, caused by your feelings, fatigue, self-confidence level, childhood issues, and so forth.

If you're feeling tired and cranky, you may think that the guy who cut in front of you in line is part of a national conspiracy to make you late and start yelling at him. When I went to an estate sale with a friend, a tired and exasperated man did something just like that. We all had been waiting for more than half-hour in a long line to make our purchases. My friend stepped over to see something in a better light, and when he got back in line next to me, the gentleman behind us started yelling at my friend, saying he had been waiting and that my friend shouldn't cut in line. When my friend said he was with me and had just stepped out of line to see something in the light, the gentleman apologized. He said he was so mad at how slow the line was moving, he didn't notice the two of us were together.

How many times have you misinterpreted a situation because you were upset, tired or irritated? Pay attention to what's going on with you. Bring your attention level up at those times when you might be most likely to misinterpret.

What is the topic or situation?

The second consideration is the topic or situation. Some topics just naturally create strong emotions and responses. I remember a wise older person telling me when I was young, "When in mixed company, never discuss religion, sex or politics." Religion, sex and politics or death are what we call "trigger" topics. You may get certain feelings just reading those words. Well, during a conversation, those trigger words can cause you or the other person to have certain body language responses. For example, if someone starts talking about Catholic priests and you have strong feeling about Catholicism (one way or the other), it can get you riled up, your body may tense, and your ability to read others can go down. That kind of response is not as likely when you're talking about the weather. When it comes to reading body language, be awake and aware when you are discussing hot topics.

One of the courses I teach is how to give effective performance appraisals. Both the possible topic (things the employee did wrong) and the situation (job security, pay, or respect) make performance appraisals hot topics. Think about a performance appraisal you either have given or have gotten. Have you noticed that people giving performance appraisals are more focused and worried about what they will say and "getting through it" rather than paying attention and responding to the employee's body language appropriately? That has been my experience. Again, this is when your focus should go up.

Obviously, when you are in a new situation, you will be paying more attention to nonverbal communication. Let's say you are walking to an office to pick up some brochures. Your attention will probably be on "low." However, if you're walking into an office for your first day at work, then it would be high. The timing of the event changes the situation. If you are out grocery shopping in your own neighborhood, your body language superpowers are pretty much on automatic pilot. Now imagine you are a tourist going down crowded Broadway in New York. You would read people with much more attention.

One time I was traveling in Ecuador with a friend. Very few people spoke English, and I did not speak Spanish, so my attention was already on full alert because I was getting all my information via nonverbal communication. We were often the only tourists I noticed on the streets. We stuck out, and I felt vulnerable. One particular day, my friend was leading me through the city to a famous statue. The buildings along our path began getting more decrepit, the streets narrower, quieter, and empty of people. As we walked further, my friend wanted to enter a dark alley. Along the alleyway, I saw a few shabbily dressed men leaning up against the walls, observing us. The situation looked and felt dangerous to me. My friend was oblivious to this; he was intent on getting to the statue before sunset. When I stopped in front of the alley, he started to pull me with him, but I pulled back and said, "No." My friend said, "Don't be silly. I'm sure it's safe." I didn't budge.

As we stood there, another, better-dressed man who spoke English came up to us and said, "Do not go down that way. It is dangerous." The situation called for super powers, and I used them. Use your super powers of nonverbal observation when the situation calls for it.

What other people are you with?

The other consideration for revving up your super powers is the person or people you are with. Your boss may require you to pay more attention to body language than the guy at the hotel check-in desk would, your two-year-old child will definitely require more attention than your neighbor. A single mother I knew was once sitting at an outside café with her 18-month-old child and the man she planned to marry. The man had just come from a bad day at work and was complaining, but the woman didn't seem to be listening because she was keeping her eyes on her child playing on the ground. Finally, in exasperation, the man asked if he was boring her. The woman had heard every word he'd said, but she didn't dare take her eyes off her child in case the toddler decided to wander off. Her fiancé obviously didn't realize the importance of her paying attention to the child's body language, and the woman wound up marrying someone else. The mother knew you have to rev up your super powers to read children.

> *Tip:* You may need to tell people that you have revved up your super powers so they know why you are acting in a particular way. My boyfriend in Ecuador and the mother's fiancé didn't know why we were acting in a particular way. As you begin using your super powers don't assume others will understand. Clear communication is critical.

Once you have decided how much conscious attention to give to a person, then you can interpret.

What is the context?

Let's say your boyfriend or girlfriend cancels your Saturday night plans. If the context of your relationship was that it was an honest one with an established trust-level, you probably would not rev up your super powers and look for deception cues. If some of the cues he gave you looked like he was nervous or tired, you could rely on the context of the relationship to tell you he is nervous and tired. Now let's say you did not trust this person. Perhaps, he or she had lied before and this was the third date that was canceled. Then you would turn on your super powers and start LOADING.

Once you have decided how much conscious attention to give according to context and situation, you can rev up you super powers when needed and start to interpret using the LOADED method.

As we go through the method you may say, "This seems complicated." Let me assure you that you already make these kinds of assessments thousands of times each day.

When a coworker gives you a big smile, makes friendly, extended eye contact and waves you toward a seat in her office, you enter and sit down in the seat. When you notice your baby making loud yum-yum noises, joyfully pounding her little spoon, quickly bouncing her feet up and down, and staring intently at the applesauce jar, you feed her more applesauce instead of carrots. When you are at the grocery store and you see two cashiers' lines are about the same length, but one cashier is smiling, pushing the groceries through quickly and has lots of service buttons on her vest, you choose her line. In each case you are looking at multiple cues in context, analyzing them and making a decision.

Personal quirks

My friend Steve has a tendency to cover his mouth with his hand when listening to another person. If you're talking to him and you notice this, you might think he is not listening to you or if he does it when he is speaking, he is lying to you. And if that is the case, he may not be the kind of person you want to have a conversation with! After all, why would you want to hang out with someone who doesn't listen or hides things from you?

So many people focus on one action and miss the other messages the person is giving them. They forget that each person has a body language cues distinctive to them. Personal quirks if you will. These quirks are motivated by the history of the person, their physical body and what going on with them in their lives and the particular day you are interacting with them. Steve has Attention Deficit Disorder and so has a tendency to impulsively interrupt or inject his own statement or point of view into the conversation. Steve found himself unconsciously placing his hand over his mouth when someone else was talking so he could suppress the urge to speak out of turn. This cue so distinctive to Steve symbolically means I would like to say something, but I do not want to interrupt you, so I will put my hand over my mouth to suppress it.

So how do you know it's just a little personal habit. How do you know that Steve wants to listen and tell the truth? Look at the full message and the context.

If you look at Steve's eyes while he does this, you'll notice he makes great eye contact. If you look at his posture, you'll find his heart is open and he is leaning toward the person speaking. He nods his head and makes excited "umm" noises. The rest of the gesture cluster shows complete attention — so you learn that the hand over the mouth means "I do not want to interrupt you." Read the whole body and notice when people have distinctive habits.

I have a wonderful friend Doug who also used to have a personal quirk of covering his mouth. I noticed when he did it and it gave me great insight into his psyche. He only covered his mouth with his hands when he was talking in a group of three people or more. Speaking in groups made him nervous. We talked about it and he said that he was such a "techie" he was afraid he would sound nerdy or stupid. There is a great ending to this story. Doug stopped this habit when he met and fell in love with his wife. She always looked at him with such love and admiration I think it gave him confidence.

You may have a habit of your own that people may be misinterpreting. Start with the cue we have been discussing. Think of all the times you cover your mouth. You may cover your mouth and laugh when someone trips going up to the stage to receive an award. You'd be covering your laughter with your hand because it is inappropriate for the event. You may cover your mouth when your boss is speaking to stifle a yawn because you're bored and you do not want your boss to know. You may cover your mouth when you tell your boyfriend that you only had a drink with the girls from work to hide the truth that it was four drinks with a guy. Or, you may cover your mouth to stop yourself from interrupting the other person.

Sometimes it is hard for others to figure out what our signals mean, but the people who know us really well can read the context signs instantly. My sweetie knows that if I raise my eyebrows and put my hand over my mouth as we start to pull out of the driveway, I've forgotten something. Without me saying a word, he pulls back into the driveway, stops the car and says. "What did you forget, honey?"

Exercise

Do you have a personal quirk? When do you use it most often? Do people misinterpret your quirk?

Please take this self-test before reading the chapter on First Impressions.

As you are answering this self-test, consider all your initial interactions with others. For example, meeting a client for the first time, buying something from a store clerk, sitting next to someone on a plane or talking to someone new at party.

1. What non-verbal factors do you examine to form a first impression? (Please be descriptive.) After each factor, describe what you think it means.

   a.

   b.

   c.

2. What is the single most important personality characteristic you look for when you meet someone

   a. In business?

   b. In a social setting?

3. In the last 7 days how many people have you met and immediately liked? (Please circle)

   a. none   less than 2   3-4   4-6   More than 6

   b. Did these people have anything in common? Yes ___ No ___

   c. If Yes, what?

4. In the last 7 days how many people have you met and immediately disliked? (Please circle)

   a. none   less than 2   3–4   4–6   More than 6

   b. Did these people have anything in common? Yes ___ No ___

   c. If Yes, what?

5. Have you ever met someone (with no prior knowledge of them) and immediately thought, "This person is going to be difficult"? Yes ___ No ___

   a. On what did you base that first impression?

   b. How accurate were you? (Circle your answer.)

Not Accurate	Somewhat Accurate	Accurate	Very Accurate	Extremely Accurate
1	2	3	4	5

6. Briefly describe the most memorable first impression situation you have experienced thus far.

7. Have you ever fallen in love at first sight? Yes ___ No ___

8. What other comments or observations or questions do you have surrounding first impressions?

9. How accurate do you believe your first impressions of others are? (Circle the number)

Not Accurate	Somewhat Accurate	Accurate	Very Accurate	Extremely Accurate
1	2	3	4	5

Chapter 4

Getting and Giving First Impressions

SAL WAS ATTENDING A COMPANY CONFERENCE WHEN HE MET JIM. They immediately hit it off and by lunchtime, Sal asked Jim to join him. He spent the entire lunch talking about an idea he had for expanding sales in their region.

After the conference, Sal went home and excitedly told his wife about this guy he met who he really liked and that he asked the guy to work with him on his new idea. Sal's wife asked, "What did you like about the guy?" Sal said, "I don't know. I just liked him."

At the same time, Jim was sitting on a plane on his way home. He was already thinking about how he and Sal could work together. He smiled as he thought of how they just clicked, but a part of him was wondering, "Why?"

Whatever the reason, both Jim and Sal got a first impression from each other that will forever be set in concrete and will influence every interaction they have.

First impressions are immediate

How often do we hear someone say, "From the moment I met him, I knew…" or "She did not fool me for a minute" or "When I first met him, I thought…"? The first impression process takes just a few seconds. In fact, the most current research says that we can form an accurate first impression in a fortieth of a second. That is not a lot of time — it's well before you've exchanged conversation or had the chance to pass out résumés. When we meet somebody, watch them on video, look at a face on a photograph, and even when we interact with somebody for the first time on the phone, we make first impressions of that person. We notice things we don't even know we notice, and those things we notice will influence our relationship forever.

Seconds or fractions of seconds for that whole categorization and assessment process would seem at first woefully inadequate and inaccurate, except for one thing — our ability to read body language. Everything you see, hear, and observe in those first few seconds is processed by your brain and mixed into a neat little package called the first impression.

Don't worry about what you say

Hector and Mark went to their local watering hole where Hector was supposed to meet Maria, his girlfriend. As they arrived, Hector told Mark that Maria was bringing a friend, Jennifer. About 15 minutes after they arrived at the tavern, Hector spotted Maria and Jennifer walking through the door. Mark noticed that Jennifer had long, black hair, and a face that Da Vinci might have preferred to the Mona Lisa. Mark was literally stunned.

In this speechless state, Mark fretted over what he would say to make a good first impression. He needn't have worried. His words were not going to be that important.

When it comes to first impressions, nonverbal cues have a heavier influence than verbal cues, more than four times the impact, according to current research. Words give us an idea of a person's future actions but the nonverbal cues tell us about a person as an individual. Each part of the body sends nonverbal communication that contributes to the first impression.

When we are face-to-face with someone, we can see his expressions, the look in his eyes, where his head is placed, the way he is sitting, his physical distance, and the animation in his gestures. We can hear, for example, the tenderness or coolness in his voice as well.

Look at faces for the most accurate assessment of someone's emotions — facial cues rank first among all forms of communication in their influence on initial impressions. In a person's eyes we see interest and arousal; in her gestures and posture we can understand what attitudes she holds, her level of confidence and what type of relationship she may want to have; and the amount of space she uses and keeps between her and others helps us assess how much privacy she wants and how close she wants to be. We listen to the words to ascertain personality and honesty; we watch the hands and touch movements to see how supportive the person is.

According to research, the impressions of personality we get from assessing nonverbal cues are extremely accurate. In fact they have been measured to an accuracy of 80% or higher. There are four reasons for this accuracy:

- We create self-fulfilling prophecies. We assign someone personality traits in the first few minutes and then as we interact, we collect information to make our predictions about that person seem true.

- There is a genetic link between appearance and personality. We may have evolved to show our personality on our faces and bodies because being more easily and accurately read makes it easier for people to socialize and interact, which is essential for survival. Just as Gila monsters develop bright coloring to show they are dangerous, we have evolved for readability.

- Our facial and body expressions reflect our personalities, and over time they form lasting facial features and body postures.

- We form first impressions subconsciously and automatically, using body language so they are not subject to conscious prejudices and are more accurate.

How the brain processes nonverbal cues

Just as we mentioned that the brain releases chemicals that determine your body language, the brain also processes the information you see and hear to create a first impression, whether during the first time we meet, or the first time we see someone on a particular day. We process these nonverbal cues in the primitive, instinctual part of the brain.

This processing does not occur in logical steps. In fact, it's messy.

Usually, when you arrive at a conclusion, you do it through a series of logical steps and can trace the mental process that you took. You can say, first this happened, then this, and then I thought this. It's linear thinking.

Processing nonverbal communication is as far from linear thinking as you can get. Most of the time, we cannot trace the steps we used to process the myriad cues available to us. Rather, the cues explode around us like Fourth of July fireworks or swirl before our eyes like floats and balloons at Macy's Thanksgiving Day Parade. We cannot always fully understand how we arrived at a conclusion. Therefore, we may not think the conclusion is accurate, and we discount it, saying, "Oh, it's only a hunch." In reality, our "hunches" may be more accurate than we realize, because they are based on a multitude of subconsciously recorded or noted nonverbal cues.

Phillip Goldberg, in his book The Intuitive Edge, says that intuition "is the product of the mind's capacity to do many things at once without our being aware of them." We can process up to 10,000 units of nonverbal information in less 40 seconds of communication — that is 10,000 nonverbal cues communicated by a person in less than a minute. Our ability to process that information into something valuable (intuition) quickly is astounding. The sheer volume of cues makes our first impressions pretty reliable.

Think about it. If we totally disregarded the nonverbal cues, we would only have a few words or perhaps sentences in those first moments on which to base our impression. I don't know about you, but "Hello, my name is Joe" does not tell me a lot. Then consider how quickly and accurately we use these nonverbal cues. In 1992, the researchers Ambady and Rosenthal found that looking at short examples of behavior (under 30 seconds) can provide predictions as accurate as those based on observing behavior for four-to-five minutes.

Forming a gut-level first impression is the first step in communicating; it dictates the reaction we expect to get, how we will relate to the other person and all the other factors that affect how we form a relationship.

Now, you may be saying, "I never make assumptions based on first impressions. I'm more sophisticated than that. I know better than to judge on mere appearances." And you may be right. So let me clarify.

I'm not talking about reducing people to stereotypes based on prejudice or bigotry. I'm talking about the accuracy of your first gut-level reactions. There is a big difference. Gut-level instinctual impressions based on nonverbal cues are natural; prejudice and bigotry stem from cultural and social factors. They are part of our second-stage impressions. True gut-level first impressions are not subject to the same inaccuracies as stereotypes.

It is impossible not to make first impressions.

It's a matter of survival

The cavemen knew all about first impressions. They would walk around looking for food when suddenly a stranger from an unfamiliar tribe would appear. The caveman had to make a very quick assessment — "Is that thing going to kill me?" Yes, we can trace the ability to form accurate first impressions to our primeval origins when we needed to protect ourselves from strangers who might be dangerous. Forming quick first impressions is one of our basic survival instincts. When our ancestors saw a stranger from an unfamiliar tribe, they had to decide quickly how to approach him or whether to approach him at all, all on the strength of first impressions. If they were not accurate, they did not survive nor did their gene pool. Research indicates we are actually genetically predisposed to form quick, accurate first impressions.

Guess what — we still need to protect ourselves.

We still have a fear of the unknown. When we meet a stranger, we're unsure of how to interact with him — we don't know his temperament or opinions. In a sense, we don't know if he bites. So we very quickly assess him. We may start by placing him in a category of safe or unsafe, and respond accordingly. This is vitally important for our comfort in a peopled world. If we could not do this, it would be too scary to leave the house at all. We'd be living on pizza and Chinese food left at the door. Even dealing with people on the phone would cause untold stress. Oh my gosh, she might yell at me and tell me I can't have pepperoni and extra anchovies. I'd better e-mail in my order.

In modern day-to-day situations, first impressions still play a critical but poorly understood role. We need them not only to know it is safe to approach, but how we should approach and interact with others. If someone comes into work harrumphing and rolling his eyes, stands in front of you with his arms crossed and growls, "Good morning," you immediately form a first impression. For one thing, you know it's not going to be a good morning as long as you have to deal with this unhappy person. You know to tread lightly or you might get your head snapped off.

If your new boss is processing paperwork and doesn't even raise her eyes towards you as you walk into her office, much less rise to shake hands, she is sending you nonverbal cues that what she is doing is more important than you are. It is going to take a lot of work to warm her up.

If a group of people at a social event is standing in a circle talking to one another and someone raises his eyebrows as you approach, smiles and steps aside to let you in, they show they are harmless and indicate their acceptance of you. You know it is safe to approach and join the circle.

These simple examples show the importance of first impressions, but for those first gut-level impressions to be useful, you have to pay attention to them.

Many years ago, I walked into a drugstore near my house and saw a tall man with a mustache wearing a well-tailored, three-piece suit and holding an unlit thin cigar as he stood nonchalantly near the magazine racks. Every fiber of my being screamed out: "Danger, danger! Will Robinson, leave the store now!" There was something about him I didn't trust. But I ignored that first impression. "This is a well dressed man," I thought. "You're being ridiculous." So I walked past him into the store and did my shopping. When I went up to the front counter with my items, the well-dressed man was in front of me checking out. Again, my whole body seized up and sent the message: "Danger! Leave now." Again, I ignored it, but I thought of something I had forgotten and left the counter to go to the rear of the store. When I returned the man was gone, and the cashier stood white-faced and frozen behind the counter. I reached out and said, "Honey, what's wrong?" She answered, "That man just robbed me at gunpoint."

Research proves that while we need to make categories to understand our world, we need to be careful of stereotypes. Stereotypes are maladaptive forms of categories. They do not correspond to what is actually present or going on in the environment. In my case, the fact that he was well dressed had no bearing on whether or not he was a gun-wielding robber.

The moral of the story? Go with your gut. Even though I am an expert in body language, I ignored my first gut-level intuition of danger because it did not make logical sense. However, my subconscious mind was busy picking up on the little nonverbal details that told me the guy in the suit was not harmless. I'd had many instances of reading people with eerie accuracy at a first meeting, but this event reminded me always to pay attention to the powerful intelligence hidden away in the subconscious mind.

The stereotype of a well-dressed gentleman was not accurate. My gut-level impression had said "danger." To this day I'm not sure why, but had I not gone to another part of the store to get something else, I might have been a statistic.

HALOES AND PITCHFORKS

Have you ever met someone, immediately liked him and then gone on to have a warm relationship with that person? Have you ever met someone and immediately said, "Don't like him, don't trust him," and later you said to yourself that you were right about the person. If so, then you have experienced the halo effect and the devil effect.

In business, for example, after we take those first few seconds to size up someone, we spend the rest of the time gathering information to justify and confirm our impression. Every person does it. There's nothing wrong with that. The difference is whether we remain unaware of how that first impression affects our relationships. If we meet someone and get good vibes, we may create a "halo effect" around her. It is a self-fulfilling prophecy. After that, every time she smiles at us, makes eye contact, or turns her heart towards us, we may note it and say, "What a friendly person." We may ignore or discount the negative nonverbal cues such as her snapping fingers and barking out orders to the waiter by rationalizing, "Oh, the waiter wasn't paying attention to us."

Attraction and the Halo effect

We often see the halo effect in our positive impressions of attractive people. Research shows we believe that "what is beautiful is good." But what determines what we think of as "beautiful"?

Here are some characteristics considered beautiful in Western cultures: childlike facial features, such as high eyebrows, small wide noses, and proportionally larger eyes and lips, as well as large heads in proportion to the body.

We also prefer facial symmetry — a balance measured from the nose to either side. In addition, we look at how straight a person's profile is, as well as the overall proportion of facial features. Halle Berry, Julia Roberts and Denzel Washington all fit our ideal of the beautiful face.

When we meet someone we find attractive, our impression of that person is generally much more positive than for those we find unattractive. Research shows us several things about this: We are more likely to like someone we find attractive and perceive them as happier and more sociable. Positive and more lasting impressions of attractive people affect how they are treated by teachers, juries, college admissions committees, managers, and job interviewers. As you might have guessed, we tend to have negative impressions of those we find unattractive. We will discuss the effects of physical and vocal attractiveness and the exceptions to them in more detail in Chapter 12.

Physical attractiveness is not the only factor in creating the halo effect. Sometimes the cues are so subtle that a positive impression seems like something magical.

WHERE ARE YOUR WINGS?

As I came down the steps of the hotel to meet the other speakers, I saw one particular woman in the crowd. She had dark hair and olive skin, big eyes and a wide smile. I knew immediately we would be friends for life. That is the story of my meeting my dear friend, Elaine. I have heard hundreds of people tell me an almost identical story when I ask in my programs, "Have you ever met someone and immediately liked them?" Yes, we do meet people whom we instantly like, and the "halo effect" can make us continue to collect good impressions about them to confirm how right we are. I have spent eighteen years as Elaine's friend and haven't found one thing wrong with her yet. These special relationships can seem magical. People describe meeting lifelong friends and feeling as if they recognized the other person the first time they saw them. I love that.

You Devil You

On my first day of graduate school, I was waiting in the parking lot to turn into a space someone was vacating. Though my signal was blinking my intention to take the space, a car swerved from behind me to steal it. This parking-space robber hopped out of her car, smiled, laughed, then shrugged her shoulders, turned away from me quickly and proceeded into the building. Minutes later, this same woman stood in front of me and the other new graduate students and gave her introductory speech. Do you think I was impressed by her gorgeous smile, her nice suit or high-energy presentation? No way! I had already formed a "devil effect" first impression when she took my parking space, then laughed with glee at her behavior. She couldn't just shrug it off.

Stealing someone's property, in this case a parking space, is a big thing. I read her behavior in conjunction with her smile, laugh, and shrug, walking away and ignoring my obvious displeasure as follows: she didn't want to be late to her speech and didn't care whom she hurt to get what she wanted. I observed these behaviors in the parking lot and my gut said, "Inconsiderate and selfish." When she didn't come up later in class and apologize, the impression stuck. Her behavior confirmed the "devil effect." I rarely dislike people, yet I was convinced I was right and found myself looking for information throughout that week that confirmed my first impression. And that impression stuck through the next year we taught together in the Speech department.

Exercise

1. Notice how you form impressions of strangers. What you would think if the rude person standing next to you in the checkout line ended up as your new boss?
2. Write down a time when someone created a halo effect and a devil effect. Include all the details you remember. What did the other person's body do? What did his or her voice sound like? Was it loud? Was it soft? Did he or she speak at a fast tempo or a slow one? Did the actions match the words? Write down what you did and how you felt about that person.

Creating a First Impression

Obviously, it doesn't take you very long to size someone up, but guess what? They're sizing you up at the same time. That means you need to pay attention to how you present yourself to others.

The first impressions people form of us are heavily influenced by our nonverbal communication. When I put out my Popsicle-cold hands to greet someone, I often make a funny comment to counteract the negative impact, like, "My warmth's in my heart, not my hands." When I go to pull up my pantyhose in the ladies room before a speech, I might want to joke with the women who see me because they might be in my audience, and say, "Don't you just hate these things!" Prepare for your first impression. Think of whom you will meet and what you want them to think about you. The four most important factors to consider in managing others' impressions of you are credibility, likeability, attractiveness, and level of dominance.

Years ago, one of my training assignments took place at a law enforcement officer-training center, where I would experience the thrill of speaking to a large group of men with guns. There I learned an important lesson in first impressions. I was a short, blond "girl" and was to spend two weeks, from 8 to 5 each day, with a group of veteran law enforcement officers instructing them on how to teach. I walked into the room with the head of the training center, and as he introduced me, I stood relaxed, leaning against the table in front of the room. Then I sat on the table, legs hung casually over the edge, and began speaking in a calm voice as I casually asked them what they wanted from this class. The class and I clicked, and we all had a great time.

Later I learned from one of the guys that before class started they got together in the parking lot and planned a full day of razzing me and trying to get me to dismiss them early that afternoon. From the written description they had received before the program, they had already pinned me as a "hoity-toity" female college instructor. But when I came in "so easy going" with the nonverbal behavior of relaxed arms, soft posture and calm voice, they wanted to be nice. Considering some of them were going to be teaching us S.W.A.T. techniques and how to fire and break down M-16s, I was more than a little relieved I'd made a good first impression. I also learned that the last female who had spoken to the group had left the first day in tears, vowing never to return. Preconceptions, in this case based on my gender and their past experiences, affected how they planned to treat me. Which of the four impression factors do you think saved me?

I haven't always been so lucky with others' first impressions. Once as I was sitting at the head table on a stage in front of 700 engineers, the emcee leaned over and mentioned he had forgotten my introduction. While others were eating lunch, I took out some paper and wrote out my introduction. Later, after giving my speech, I learned that the audience had watched me writing and thought I was composing my speech at the last minute. This affected my credibility. Many formed a negative first impression that I luckily changed fairly quickly when I started my presentation by dashing off the stage and into the audience without any speech notes. I could have really blown it. As it was, I had to overcome a negative first impression formed before I even got up to speak.

How we form a first impression:

- Clothing and artifacts (accessories, jewelry, etc.)
- Facial expressions
- Voice
- Body (posture, movement)
- Gestures
- Use of space

A few fun facts about first impressions

When we see someone who has a baby face, we ascribe to that person characteristics of submissiveness, naiveté, honesty, kind-heartedness, weakness and warmth. When we see someone with mature-faced characteristics, we attribute adult characteristics to the person. A good example of the use of facial maturity on impressions is how the characteristics of Mickey Mouse and Bugs Bunny have changed over the years.

Mickey Mouse has been drawn to look much younger than he originally was, with a bigger head and bigger eyes. We see him as more charming and endearing. On the other hand, Bugs Bunny's head has gotten smaller and his eyes have gotten narrower, and we see him as more abrasive and clever.

Have you ever noticed how quickly and effectively children size up a stranger? Children rely on their gut instincts. Rather than being distracted by the words, they pay attention to the nonverbal communication and that can make them very people-savvy. Children have not formed the stereotypes and prejudices that we have as adults. They don't have all those life experiences — the heartbreaking first love, the mean boss, the obsessive high school teacher with the red pen — to clog up their filter system and create stereotypes and categories.

The same thing goes for pets. Pets can make accurate assessments of people and situations because animals are astute readers of body language. They don't have the language skills to decipher much of what we're saying. They pay much more attention to your nonverbals. For instance, if you've ever seen the "horse whisperer" on television, then you've seen how he uses body language to train horses. Most domesticated animals are quite fluent in body language.

Brian Hare, a Harvard biological anthropologist, conducted a study comparing dogs to chimpanzees in their ability to "read" humans. Guess which species was more accurate? Fido won, paws down. Dogs picked up information from the subtlest hand gestures and even understood the meaning of a human glance. The chimps didn't have a clue.

"It looks like there's been direct selection for dogs with the ability to read social cues in humans," Hare said, confirming that centuries of selective breeding have created an animal that knows us better than our closest primate cousins do.

When I was teaching at Florida State University, I was given a dog that had been abandoned by some college students. "Boss Dog" was extremely loyal and was always by my side. Whenever I would go to the door to meet my date for the evening, I could always tell by Boss's response exactly the kind of date I was going to have. If the dog responded positively to the man, I would too! I called Boss my "date-ometer." I am sure that Boss was not only picking up on my date's nonverbal cues, but on my subtle cues in response to the man as well. I might not be aware of those cues or be able to wag my tail, but Boss sure could.

First impressions are sticky

Not only do we form first impressions very quickly, but also, according to research, it can take up to six months of constant interaction to change an incorrect first impression. That's kind of scary. Think about it. That means that if you meet someone who for some reason doesn't like you, it may take that person six months to change his mind and realize you're a wonderful human being. That's the power of the "primacy effect." We have a tendency to give more weight to our first impression of a person than to our later impressions. The primacy effect means the first impression may affect all future thoughts about the person and it is very resistant to change.

Over and over, impression research indicates that what we initially see in others and what they see in us tends to be remembered. That makes it imperative for you to form good, accurate first impressions.

Exercise

1. Think back over your history. Has there been a time when preconceptions affected how others saw you? How has your unconscious initial behavior affected another's first impression of you? (Don't think about your attire — we will discuss that later.) Have you been in a hurry or busy when you first met someone? How do you think it affected your impressions of one another?

2. Think of a particular time when someone formed a first impression of you that you discovered was inaccurate. Perhaps it was a date who later said that he thought differently of you after spending more time with you, or a colleague who was initially biased against another person coming in the workgroup. Think back and ask yourself what were your nonverbal behaviors at the first meeting? Which of the four impression factors — credibility, likeability, attractiveness, and level of dominance were affected?

3. Since we not only form first impressions of strangers but also form them at the beginning of interactions in which we have not seen each other for a certain period of time, consider your morning work rituals and/or your evening coming-home- to- family rituals. When and how do you greet others? How do you think your nonverbal greeting affects their impression of you?

Exercise 11

Ask yourself: What are my three best qualities?

1.

2.

3.

How do I express these qualities nonverbally?

Do people know that I possess those qualities when they first meet me?

Chapter 5

Second-Stage Impressions

A FRIEND OF MINE I KNOW LOVES TO TELL A FUNNY STORY ABOUT when she met her husband. She and her mother differed in their opinions about his personality. Karen's husband, Marty is a highly gregarious guy, talks a lot, and tends to be a little louder than most, especially when around lots of people. If he was talking, he couldn't keep his body still, his arms flailing all over the place, putting emphasis on his words. When Karen met him, he had a devil-may-care attitude that was, in its way, somewhat charming. This being the early 1970s, he didn't worry too much about how neat his hair was, or whether his clothes were clean or torn. Karen fell for him quickly, treasuring his individuality and his ability to make people laugh.

In the early stages of their relationship, Karen was living at home with her Mom and Dad and would invite friends over from time to time. When her friends were over, her new boyfriend tended to be the "life of the party," and his voice could be heard throughout the house.

Her mom, on the other hand, valued order and, to a great extent, quiet. Mom was clearly the queen of the house and liked things the way she liked them. The house was neat, clean, and ordered.

About three months into the relationship, Karen noticed that her mom didn't join the conversation when it involved anything about Marty. One day, Karen confronted her mother about Marty. "Do you have a problem with Marty?" Karen asked.

"I don't know what you see in him or how you can care about him. He has no self-respect. He doesn't care about the way he looks, doesn't care about whether his clothes are clean, and he's obnoxious," her mom rambled. "Obnoxious?" Karen asked. "When has he ever been obnoxious to you or Dad?

"He hasn't been obnoxious to me in particular, but listen to how loud he is. Can't he control his volume? I'm not deaf, you know." Her mom also felt that Marty spent too much time talking to other people and didn't pay enough attention to Karen. The thought had never occurred to Karen that Marty was that type of person. In fact, everything her mom hated about Marty, Karen loved.

In the eye of the beholder

What you see when you encounter another person may differ from what someone else notices. After the first ninety seconds of interacting with someone, what we look for may be related to what we value and hold important rather than just "safety" features. Like a huge air filter sorting out pollutants, you begin to make associations between the nonverbal behaviors you witness and the inner qualities you believe they reflect. Then you separate the people you want to continue to interact with from those you don't. In this second-stage assessment, we filter everything we see and hear through our own personal experiences and biases and assign a type — as in stereotype — to them. Studies show the longer you consciously deliberate using those preferences and judgments, the less accurate and predictive they become. Again, most research says second stage impressions are accurate less than 30% of the time.

I do an exercise in my workshops that I want you to do right now. Ask yourself what you believe to be the most important quality another person can have. What characteristic or kind of personality do you value above all others?

Think about it and write it down now. Now write down the second and third most important qualities:

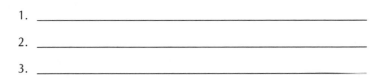

1. _____

2. _____

3. _____

Having done this exercise with thousands of people over the last 20 years, I have been amazed at the similarity of the answers among very different groups of people. From police officers to accountants, teachers to engineers, college students to secretaries, the answers are the same. The number one answers are usually: "trustworthy," "real," "sincere," "honest." Or they will respond with phrases such as "they are just what you see" and "nothing phony." This makes sense, as those are the characteristics related to gut-level impressions of a person's harmlessness and predictability.

The number two answers include "kind," "considerate," "polite," "sensitive" — values again related to whether someone is safe to be around. And the number three answers include "predictable," "reliable," "someone you can count on" and other related words and ideas. People ask themselves: "Can I trust him? Does she care? Can I count on him?"

Some of the answers differ by gender; women often say they value a good sense of humor, someone who laughs easily, and men often say they look for someone who has a firm handshake or is confident and well groomed. Other answers are highly personal, such as "a good listener" or "someone who likes children." These values affect our first impressions. Again, think back to the four factors that most affect our impressions: credibility, likeability, interpersonal attractiveness and dominance.

PAY ATTENTION

Pay attention to your first gut-level impressions and second-stage impressions. If you talk to someone new on the phone, write down some thoughts about him or her in your notes. If you meet someone and exchange business cards, write down your first impression of him on the back. Go back to your notes later and check for accuracy.

You'll notice as you begin to check for accuracy how your value system affects what you see in other people at that second stage of assessment. Whatever you hold as being important — what you feel is most like you — acts as a screen for your judgment of others. For example, the first thing I notice about a person is whether she's sincere. If I'm talking to someone who does not look at me with full, connecting eye contact, who has her head turned toward me but not her heart, whose words sound nice and gooey but whose nonverbal are closed off, I perceive that person as not being real. I place her in the "be careful" category. Then I begin to investigate what she might be hiding.

While sitting at a banquet table at an association event, I watched the former association president pick up my iced tea glass and begin drinking. I thought, "Oh, that's sweet. He didn't notice that glass was mine." His mistake actually humbled him and endeared him to me. To his right sat an expert and professional speaker on business etiquette. She said to him, "You just drank from Patti's glass!" She later told me how appalled she was at his bad manners and that a person of his stature should know that beverages are to your right.

These differing reactions demonstrate how personal factors affect how we assess someone else's behavior. My first impression of him was great. I thought, "He's just an ordinary person like me. Who watches to see which glass to use?" She thought he was a complete oaf. I valued someone for being real; she valued proper etiquette. Both values are equally valid but they led to different impressions. We form our values in our cognitive brains and we base them on the cultural and social factors I mentioned before. That means these second-stage impressions can be inaccurate and affected by stereotypes and prejudice, so be wary.

According to a 1982 study by Don E. Hamachek, three principles most affect second-stage impressions:

- We tend to give more weight to negative information than positive information. My colleague ignored all the president's positive cues — his warm smile, his gentle voice, and the way he would lean forward and make eye contact while listening to another person. She only saw the etiquette rule breaking.
- We tend to be influenced by what's most obvious — drinking out of the wrong glass was pretty obvious.
- We tend to judge others on the assumption that most people are like us, or should be like us. My colleague would never break a rule of etiquette and expected others to follow those same rules.

As you can see, your specific value system affects the way you read people. And your impressions of others say as much about you as they do about the people you're assessing.

Exercise

Write down your first impression of the next three people you meet, either in person or over the phone.

What impression-factor(s) are you using? What is your assessment of each one and what is the principle behind your assessment? List as many nonverbal behaviors as you can think of, including voice, gestures, etc. For example:

Clothing and artifacts (or accessories): _____

    Thought: _____

    Impression-factor: _____

    Principle: _____

Clothing and artifacts (or accessories):_____

    Your Thoughts: _____

    Impression-Factors: _____

    Principle: _____

Facial Expressions: _____

    Your Thoughts: _____

    Impression-Factors: _____

    Principle: _____

Voice: _____

    Your Thoughts: _____

    Impression-Factors: _____

    Principle: _____

Body (posture, movement): _____

    Your Thoughts: _____

    Impression-Factors: _____

    Principle: _____

Analyze

- Whom have you met in your life that you immediately liked?
- What nonverbal cues did you pick up on that led you to like that person?
- How accurate was your first impression?
- Whom have you met in your life that you immediately disliked or didn't trust?
- What nonverbal cue did you pick up on that led you to dislike that person?
- How accurate was your first impression?

Explore

    Play! Try changing your normal behavior around strangers, and then do it around people who know you. Take note of their reactions.

Please Respond to the following Handshake Survey

As you are answering this survey, consider all your initial interactions with others, for example, meeting a client for the first time, buying something from a store clerk, sitting next to someone on a plane or talking to someone new at a party. If you can, please go to www.surveymonkey.com and go to Greeting Behavior Home Test on the home page.

1. Rate the following nonverbal factors you use to form a first impression with 7 being the most important and 1 being the least important.
    a. smile __   b. attractiveness __   c. eye-contact __
    d. handshake __   e. breath __   f. overall demeanor __
    g. other (specify) _____

2. What is the biggest mistake someone can make when greeting another person?

3. Which of the following do you generally prefer to have offered to you as a greeting by a person that you are meeting for the first time? (Please circle a number)

Handshake	Hug	Kiss	A greeting that does not involve physical contact (e.g., a smile)	Other
1	2	3	4	5

    If you circled 'Other' please specify: _____

4. Do you like to shake hands? Yes or No and why?
    _____

5. How would you describe the way you shake hands?
    _____

6. How does shaking hands with someone affect your interaction?
    _____

7. Do you think someone's handshake can tell you something about them? Yes __ No __
    If yes to the above, what do you think someone's handshake tells you about him/her? _____

8. What is the number one mistake a person can make when shaking hands with someone? _____

9. Have you ever been in a situation were you wanted to shake hands and did not have the opportunity? Yes __ No __
    If yes, how did you feel? _____

10. If you do not have the opportunity to shake hands, do you think it takes longer to feel comfortable with them? Yes __ No __
11. If a person did not shake hands with you even though you extended your hand to them what would you think about them?

_____

12. What would keep you from shaking hands with someone?

_____
_____

13. Would your decision to buy from someone be influenced by the type of handshake he/she gave you? Yes __ No __
    If yes, what kind of handshake would make you not buy from someone
    a. __ No palm to palm contact — that is, they grip just the ends of your fingers or arch their palm
    b. __ Palms touch but little or no pressure
    c. __ Bone crusher
    d. __ Other specify
14. How does the gender of the person you're shaking hands with affect your handshake?
15. Are you more comfortable shaking hands with a man or a woman? Why?

_____
_____

16. Which one of the following words best describes you?
    a. __ Helper
    b. __ Analyzer
    c. __ Doer
    d. __ Persuader
17. Your gender: Male __ Female __
18. Your age: (Please circle one option)
    Under 25   26–35   36–45   46–55   Over 55
19. Your nationality: _____
20. Your occupation: _____
21. Which of the following is most important to you?
    __ a. To get it right
    __ b. To get along
    __ c. To get it done
    __ d. To get appreciated

22. Which of the following paragraphs best describes you? Check one only.

___ a. You are warm and friendly and like a relaxed pace. The most important thing in your life is your relationships with others.

___ b. You are smart, careful and accurate. A deep thinker, you consider things before you speak. You are detailed and precise and catch mistakes that others miss.

___ c. Your lifestyle is fast paced and you are always on the go to get things done. You like to get things done and then move on. You take command. You are fast, decisive and to the point.

___ d. You are a leader and an influencer. You want to be noticed and appreciated for your ideas and what you do. You are spontaneous and live life to the fullest. You don't like to waste your time or energy on boring details. You are boisterous, imaginative and playful.

Chapter 6

Shake On It — Handshakes

I SPEAK AROUND THE COUNTRY TO COURT REPORTERS. COURT RE-
porters are the people, predominately women, who record every word said in
the courtroom or in a deposition. They have a lot of stories about the lawyers
they work with.

Many of them talk about a particular handshake ritual they see occur at
the beginning and end of a trial or deposition. Lawyers who have known
each other for years will come in and shake hands with each other. Then
those same lawyers will spend the entire day or trial saying horrible, deroga-
tory things about one another, shake their fists, frown and nod negatively, roll
their eyes, and express other disrespectful gestures and sounds when the other
lawyer is talking. They will, in effect, go to battle. However, when the deposition or trial is over, they will get up walk over to each other, smile, shake
hands again and say, "Let's go out for a drink." They are buddies again.

The court reporters are flummoxed. How can the guys do that? How can
you shake hands and be friends again with someone who treated you so
abominably? What they don't realize is that this is gamesmanship. The game
rules say "Shake hands with your opponent, and come out fighting." When
the game's over, the game is really over, so leave your bad feelings on the
playing field and shake hands again. This ritual is repeated by men over and
over on the sports playing field as they grow up, so in adulthood it is second
nature to them to shake hands and come out fighting.

Handshakes and first impressions

In the previous chapter, I talked about the importance of the first impression. I mentioned that you can affect the impression you make on others with some preparation. It begins the moment you walk into a room.

Not surprisingly, recent studies indicate that a firm handshake that shows strength and vigor with appropriate eye contact length and completeness of grip creates a favorable first impression. The handshake ritual is powerful and rich with symbolic significance. It's something you do without even thinking about it and it profoundly affects your relationships.

The handshake is the quickest, most effective way to establish rapport with another person. Research in the United States shows it takes an average of three hours of continuous interaction to develop the same level of rapport you get with a handshake.

Here are some of the handshake rules: Walk up to a person and give him a firm three-to-five pump handshake in greeting while standing approximately 16 inches away. In business, you greet someone in this manner and then step back to a minimum of two-and-a-half feet distance, with no other touch in the critical first four minutes of the interaction. A handshake gives you information to help you form a first impression of that person, or if you have met him before, to form an impression of him for that interaction.

When do you shake hands?

- When you are introduced
- When you say goodbye
- When an outsider visits you
- When you encounter someone outside the confines of your office
- When you enter a room or meet people you already know
- When you exit any business meeting attended by outsiders

A brief history of the handshake

In Western cultures, we use handshaking to greet another person and "seal" a contract or promise. Most historians believe that the handshake once demonstrated that neither party was about to use a weapon. Romans put out their right hand because that was their weapon hand and their left hand shielded the heart. They then grabbed each other's forearms so neither could attack. The intent was clear: handshakes were weapons checks. The vertical shaking pattern was originally used so knights could dislodge hidden weapons from another knight's sleeve — "Hey there, I like the fact you put out your hand and everything, but you might have daggers up that sleeve, so I'm going to shake for awhile and find out."

This shaking formalized the weapons check and thus disarmed aggressive impulses. Nothing up my sleeve, so let's be friends.

Why handshakes are important

A friend of mine has been a classroom trainer for more than a decade and repeatedly gets high ratings from his audiences. But early in his career, he found that it took what seemed an eternity to get the class to warm up to him and the subject at hand.

One day, a fellow trainer invited him to watch her teach a particular course. My friend sat in the back of the room and watched as his more experienced colleague made sure to greet each person who entered her classroom. She greeted each person with a handshake, introduced herself, asked for the person's name (if the person didn't automatically respond) and then repeated the person's name. She then welcomed them to the class.

My friend noticed that when the class started, his colleague seemed to have immediate rapport with the participants. He vowed to try her "handshake" technique with his next class.

The difference was astounding. By the time the class started, he felt that he'd already made a personal connection with each person in the room and they with him. Class participants started participating within 15 minutes of the class starting, whereas it used to take at least a half-hour to an hour to get them involved. He could not believe the difference. He went back to his colleague to share his observations and to ask her if she had any idea why.

"When you shake hands, you make a physical connection. That gesture, combined with great eye contact and saying their names creates a relationship before the class even begins. It's no wonder you had a better response," she told him.

We expect to shake hands

Have you ever walked into a meeting late and not had the opportunity to shake hands? Or have you gone to shake someone's hand and the person failed to reach out? How does it feel when you have to interact with someone and you didn't have that opportunity to shake hands?

My audiences report that they feel awkward, uncomfortable, disconnected, snubbed, and distant, guarded and, if it is a meeting, not part of the group. That's not surprising. We can get rapport in seconds with a handshake or we can awkwardly work for the same level of rapport over many hours. Makes you want to shake hands with everyone from now on, doesn't it?

People shake hands when they are first introduced, whenever they enter and leave a room and before and after a meeting. People would consider you impolite if you do not do so.

Although in the past few years the handshake has become the internationally accepted business greeting, North Americans and many Europeans shake hands more often than people of other cultures do. The handshake can serve as an important verb in your body language vocabulary. Few things can create such an effective first impression as an easily given, gracious handshake. In addition, the handshake can make or break a business interview or other personal encounter. The handshake changes the way we feel about the other person. We feel safer and more at ease once we have taken part in that magic bonding ritual.

When visiting my friend Michael in Paris I noticed that the handshake often preceded the cheek kiss. Michael said the handshake is very important in France and that they actually shake hands more often than Americans do. The ritual is different, the handshake is very brief, and in Paris it is often followed by the triple kiss. The handshake brings the person closer, then the person will plant a kiss on one cheek, then the other, then back to the first cheek for the final kiss. I love this. When I spent time with Michael, we would greet his friends with the triple kiss and people would leave with the kiss. Michael said that at work all meetings start with a handshake and end with a handshake and often with the cheek kiss. Though Michael found the kiss awkward when he first moved to Paris, he soon saw its advantages. "It's hard to get mad or irritated with your co-workers when you kiss them hello and goodbye everyday." Now after years as an expatriate, he says he could never go back to a culture where you do not greet each other warmly.

The handshake is also important as an indicator in male gamesmanship. Just as boxers, team captains and coaches shake hands before a competitive sporting event, men shake hands at the beginning of a business meeting to indicate that the "game" has begun and during the meeting can safely disagree and argue and even yell. At the end of the meeting, they shake hands again to show the games over and they are friends again — "Let's go out for drinks." When a woman shakes hands with a man in the correct manner, she's allowed to enter into the game.

Shaking hands is an extremely important ritual. When we shake hands, we are actually exchanging chemicals with the other person. Those chemicals, like the better-known pheromones, send a message to our brain so we get a chemical read on the other person. That makes it easier for us to remember the person and to remember the person's name.

A study on trade show handshakes done by the Income Center for Trade Shows showed that people are two times more likely to remember you if you shake hands with them. The chemicals create a bond in our psyche. The trade show research also showed that people respond to those with whom they shake hands by being more open and friendly. Other research demonstrates that shaking hands makes you more likable and seem friendly. Shaking hands increases your ability to persuade others and increases the likelihood of a sale. My research shows that my friend was right: audiences listen more intently, are more polite and give a higher credibility rating to a speaker if the speaker shakes hands with them or a representative sample of the audience. In other words, it pays to shake hands!

But you're a Lady!

Remember the basis of the handshake? Handshakes are weapons checks: "Are you packing any weapons? Let me check. Nope. Okay, let's talk." This interpretation would explain why, until quite recently, it was chiefly males who practiced handshaking. For men, a strong grip signifies male bonding through a silent display of competitive power.

Can you imagine the insult in earlier times if a man would reach his hand out to a woman? "Hey, babe, I think you're packing heat, and I need to check it out." Offering one's hand to a woman would carry the outrageous implication that the "gentler sex," too, could be dangerous. (Of course, now men know that we might be, so they'd better check.) Since men are still taught, especially in the Southern United States, to wait for a woman to extend her hand before they offer theirs, women should always put out their hands first so men do not have to guess whether it is appropriate.

I recommend that men ignore the old rule and put out their hands to women when doing business in North America, except in the states of Kentucky and Tennessee, where according to my research, you still need to abide by the "southern belle" standards.

Since the shaking aspect is so much a part of the handshake ritual, I have found that men actually have a secret handshake in American culture, a secret that most women do not know. What's the secret?

Pump three to five times.

Why so many pumps? Like many male species, there is a dance of power when one male meets another. They look for nonverbal signals to see who will be the alpha male, whether one will control the meeting, or whether they will meet as equals. Men use the handshake to size each other up and they need plenty of time to do it. They need to have something going on so they can stay close and have their power contest. So they keep shaking up and down.

SHAKE HANDS? NO THANKS

Even though a handshake gives you enormous advantages, some people prefer not to shake hands. In the last few years, I have found a significantly higher proportion of respondents to my surveys saying they do not want to shake hands. The number one reason? A fear of germs.

Young people under 25 are especially fearful. Research conducted in 1997 by Market Fact, Inc. of Chicago revealed that 51 percent of Americans wish they could wash their hands after shaking another person's hand. Their survey also indicates that women are more concerned about germs than men are. While 57 percent of women wish they could wash their hands, only 44 percent of men have the same concern.

I find it funny that people are so concerned about getting germs from handshakes when so many things we touch all day long — including door handles, water facet handles, the buttons on an elevator and the keys on the copy machine — all hold germs. A memo passed around the office holds germs for up to twelve hours! But you're not going to form a close personal relationship with a door handle or a shared staple gun. Go ahead and shake hands.

I'm often called at the last minute to do media interviews, but strangely enough, I rarely get nervous. Typically, I will get an urgent call and then rush to a TV studio to make comments about a breaking story. When I get to the studio, the producer or journalist I will be working with shakes my hand and ushers me into the studio. I sit calmly as they put a microphone on me, and we do a sound check. One day I got a call to do a read of President Bush's body language. I have done that dozen of times, so I thought it would be fun, and no big deal. When I entered the Fox news affiliate studio, I put out my hand, but the producer pulled her hand back and said, "I'm sick and don't want to give you germs." She then turned and walked ahead of me. As I walked to the studio, my heart began to race and I had to ask for water because my mouth got dry. My hands shook as I sat on the stool in front of the cameras. I started to sweat.

What was different this time? The host, or "tribal chieftain," didn't shake my hand to signal she was not going to hurt me and that the station was safe for me to enter. Without that warm greeting, I felt danger. My cave woman instincts kicked in and I had a great need for a good antiperspirant.

THE SECRET OF THE PERFECT HANDSHAKE

Few things can create such an effective first impression as an easily given, gracious handshake, but unless your father took you aside and gave you tips as a teenager, most likely no one told you the ideal way to shake hands. Based on my research, here is the best way in North American culture to have the perfect handshake:

Rise, if seated. That rule used to apply to men only, now women should rise as well. If you remain seated when someone is introduced to you, the communication of personal indifference is unmistakable, not to mention offensive. The only approved exception to rising to shake hands is if you are eating. If that is the case, you can wait to shake hands until after you are done.

Walk up to the person with confidence. Keep your head level and your hands at your side. Be sure to keep your hands out of your pockets. Research indicates that we don't trust people with hands in their pockets. Make sure your right hand is free to shake hands. Always shift any purses, briefcases, papers, beverages or cell phones to your left hand before you begin the greeting.

Smile briefly. Don't overdo it. If you smile too long or too much, they can perceive you as submissive. An over-extended smile can create negative impressions, such as "overeager," "easily manipulated" or "not intelligent." Women need to take special care not to over-extend the smile as it can reduce personal power and can even be misinterpreted as a sexual come on.

Make eye contact. There is a substantial amount of research showing that good eye contact increases feelings of trust. Don't stare, but don't look at your shoes. Making eye contact as you approach lets the person know you want to interact. Men need to extend the eye contact for at least three seconds without blinking or looking away as they shake hands. Women need to be careful of holding eye contact for more than three to five seconds at a time with men they have not met before. Men may perceive an extended eye contact as a sexual advance.

Face the person heart-to-heart. When you stand at an angle and don't face the person squarely, you are sending the symbolic message that you are not being straight and open. You may look as if you need to protect yourself, you do not like the other person or you feel the need to reduce the intimacy or the duration of the interaction.

Make sure your hands are clean and dry. If you have a problem with clammy hands, don't forget to wipe them on your handkerchief or tissue before you shake hands. At social functions, carry any iced drinks in your left hand, so your right will not be cold and damp when a handshake is called for.

Strike out your right hand and arm across your body to your left. The forcefulness and confidence of the move lets the other person know you not only want to shake hands, but that you look forward to it.

Make sure the arm goes fully outward. An arm held closely to the body indicates timidity and lack of confidence.

Offer your hand with the thumb on top. The thumb on top is symbolic — it indicates you want equality in your interaction. No one person will dominate. You will respect the other person and expect him or her to respect you.

Stretch out and open your hand between the thumb and the first finger. This insures that you can slide your hand easily into the web of the other person's hand. Make sure the rest of your fingers are together with your palm flat rather than cupped so palm can touch palm.

Make palm-to-palm contact. Open palms symbolically show a desire to be open and honest in your interactions; not giving a person contact with your palm in a handshake is read subliminally as a lack of openness and honesty. It's why we hate a wimpy handshake. It makes the other person nervous and he or she may wonder what you are hiding (If someone puts out their hand with the palm up, it shows they want to support you and may go along with your ideas. When the palm is down, it shows their power is important to them and they like to be on top and win the negotiation.)

Once full contact is made, wrap your fingers around the other person's, put your thumb down gently, lock thumbs and squeeze the hand firmly. The pressure should be equal or at the most slightly more than the pressure the other person gives. Never grip the other's hand in a contest of macho handshaking to see who can hold the hardest or longest. You want to have a firm handshake, but the rule is to match the pressure or add no more than two steps in pressure.

How to Handle Handshakes

The handshake is a potent element of your general greeting style. This is an important body language communicator, for it speaks volumes about who you really are and what you actually think. For instance, if you remain seated when someone is introduced to you, the communication of personal indifference is unmistakable, not to mention offensive. Here are some other handshake tips.

Son, Always Give a Firm Handshake

Men often tell me how their fathers taught them to shake hands. Inevitably, they say their dads emphasized having a good strong grip. A firm handshake is critical. The majority of people do not want to do business with someone who gives them a wimpy handshake. Research shows men tend to have firmer handshakes than women do and that people see individuals with firm handshakes as more extroverted and "open to experience," and less neurotic and shy. And women who are more "open to experience" have a firmer hand-shake than women who are less open.

DON'T BE A WIMP

In researching this topic over many years, I have found that even more important than the firmness of the grip is the contact of the palms. We want to make full palm-to-palm contact with the other person when we shake hands. That makes sense because when you are reading body language, you observe the palms of the hands to discover if someone is being honest with you and is willing to self -disclose. If someone shakes hands with you and gives you just her fingers and not her full palm, at a subconscious level you may think, "What is she hiding? What is she keeping from me? I do not like her. I do not trust her." It doesn't feel right.

Similarly, I have discovered that many women arch the palm of their hand when they shake hands, precluding palm-to-palm contact. They give various reasons for this such as shyness, lack of confidence in themselves or in their handshakes, or most often, not wanting men to think they are forward or giving a sexual signal. Granted palm-to-palm contact can be construed as intimate, but it is that way for a reason. It symbolically says, "I will be open with you." In fact, men say they dislike it when women arch their hands, and they characterize the woman as stuck up, rather than the shy unsure person she believes that she is.

The most important finding in my survey research is that people, espe-cially men, do not want to interact with someone who gives them a wimpy handshake and would even prefer to interact with someone who gives them a bone-crusher handshake. At least with a bone-crusher, you know what you're getting. With the wimpy handshake, there is no substantial information con-veyed.

Handling a wimpy handshake is difficult; once you are inside it, there is not much you can do, except perhaps to say, "Let's try that again." So you must use preventative measures.

I started my speaking and consulting business in Tallahassee, Florida when I was teaching at Florida State University. Tallahassee has a Southern small town culture. When I would go out to meet my prospective clients, they would often greet me with a wimpy handshake and some time during the greeting call me "little lady." This did not exactly start me off on the right foot — make that hand — with them. I wanted them to respect me and pay me lots of money. You do not do that with a wimpy handshaking little lady. It's interesting that they offered a wimpy handshake, not because they were wimpy but because they thought I was. Though they were not offering me their full-palmed, firm handshake, I wanted it.

So I developed a four-step method to prevent wimpy handshakes. Since you never know when you are going to get a wimpy handshake, use these steps each time you go to shake hands:

1. First, strike out your hand fully toward the other person. This says, "Oh baby, I can take it."
2. Then with your thumb arched away from the rest of your fingers, go in confidently, landing like a 747 and lock thumbs so the curve between your thumb and fingers is tight with theirs.
3. Make palm-to-palm contact.
4. Pump three to five times.

OUCH! MY HAND: THE BONE-CRUSHER

Have you ever had someone give you a bone-crusher handshake? You wanted to squeeze back, you really wanted to make them suffer, but you couldn't because your hand was locked in a vice grip.

People give bone-crusher handshakes for a variety of reasons. One reason is cluelessness. They have no idea that their handshake is painful. Another is simply habit. The typical handshake is an ingrained habit that has been practiced over many years. Perhaps the "bone-crusher" remembers that first rehearsal with Dad and the desire to impress him, so he maintains that emphatic grip when it is no longer appropriate. Or the bone-crusher may have low self-esteem so he compensates with a handshake that makes him look confident. A feeling of powerlessness or a fear of conflict also might cause a bone-crushing handshake because the person wishes to start the interaction aggressively in order to counteract future confrontations. Finally, it may just be a case of the BIG EGO, the "I will show you who is boss from the get go" mentality.

Sometimes, you are better off letting the bone-crusher have their thrill. But other times you really need to start the interaction on an equal footing so that each of you knows you have equal power and control. So if you get a bone-crusher handshake at the beginning of that important contract negotiation, use the following technique:

When someone gives you a bone-crusher handshake, your crushed hand is helpless to respond, but your other hand is totally free and available so you can take that free hand and wrap it around the offending hand. This sends the message, "Hey, you're surrounded. Lighten up." Interestingly, I have found that the giver of the bone-crusher handshake will not register what you have done on a conscious level. I assume that on a subconscious level, they know you are a force to be reckoned with.

Women have another response they can use with anyone. They can take their free hand and gently pat the offending hand sending the message: "bad boy" or "bad girl" and magically the man or women will ease up on the vice-like grip. However, if you are a man shaking hands with another man who gives a bone-crusher handshake, I do not recommend the patting motion. It could get you into big trouble. Instead, you can simply encompass their hand as described above.

THE TWO-HANDED HANDSHAKE

While the two-handed technique lets the other person know at a subconscious level that you are a force to be reckoned with, it may also serve other purposes. Depending on the amount of pressure, location and manner in which you position the outside hand, you can send many different messages. For example, gently resting your left hand underneath the handshake symbolically says, "I'm here to support you." You may have gotten this handshake from your doctor, minister or religious leader. Taking the left hand and placing it gently on the outside of the other person's hand as you smile warmly at them can communicate warmth and extend friendliness. It is something you see mainly in the Southern U.S. However, heavy pressure changes the dynamic into a two-handed grip so that the person not only feels surrounded, but may also feel smothered. Taking the outside hand, placing it on top of the handshake and pressing down shows the person's superiority. Top down usually communicates a power move.

The location of the left hand can also send other messages as it moves up the arm into what we call "a politician's handshake." The farther up the arm, the more the person can control and move the other person physically and symbolically. This can be important for politicians because we want politicians to have power and control over all situations. Former President Lyndon B. Johnson was famous for using this technique to box wavering senators into a corner. But when a boss or supervisor does that, thinking he is showing warmth, he is actually showing his need for control.

HANDS DOWN

You go to shake someone's hand and he puts out his hand toward you with his palm down. You are left with no option but to take his hand, leaving your hand on the bottom. Who has more power–the person with his hand on top or you on the bottom? As we mentioned before, the person on top always shows more power. However, you are not stuck on the bottom. Here is a subtle trick:

As the other person approaches with his palm down you can take the hand and shift your weight forward on your right foot in the normal hand-shaking leg movement. At the very same moment as you shift your weight, gently and quickly turn your palm half -way over as it meets the other palm, so both of you end the turn with your thumbs on top in an equal handshake. You don't need to turn all the way and put the other person on the bottom. He would notice such a shift consciously, as he would notice it if you tried to pull a Bruce Lee and flip him. Instead, just bring both hands to an equal, up-right position.

HEY, LET GO OF ME!
THE LINGERING HANDSHAKE

"So I walked in to meet him, and he wouldn't let go of my hand. Even when we stopped shaking, he just held on. It felt awful!"

The ritual of the handshake is so specific we could even count in sec-onds how long it should last. When someone does not let go, it feels bad. In man-to-man handshakes, there is an undercurrent of competition when one holds the other hand captive. There's a great scene in the remake of the movie Ocean's 11 in which a character destroys a car salesman's confidence simply by holding his hand in a lingering captive handshake.

Competitiveness can also be the case in male-to-female handshakes. However, many women report feeling that the man who does not let go of her hand in a handshake is really giving them a sexual come on. Sometimes they even feel violated by a "lingering captive" handshake.

So how do you get out of it? Well, the natural response would be to pull away with your hand or your body. But that just makes the other person hold tighter. In addition, by pulling away you show fear and weakness. Instead, follow the "Let Go, Ego" rules:

1. Shift your weight forward over your right foot (your natural handshaking foot). Don't lift your foot. Just gently shift your weight forward so that your upper body is in the other person's intimate space. You are now in the space we usually reserve for attacking others. It's a subtle attack, brief but potent, just long enough to discombobulate the other person.

2. Don't bow, bend at the waist or step forward. Bowing or bending makes you look weak, and stepping forward draws too much attention to your movement.
3. At the same time as you shift your weight, splay out your fingers and break downward. Because you have put the other person off center in the same moment with your shift, he will have momentarily loosened his grip enough for you to break out of it.
4. Shift your weight back again. If you linger in the attack zone, the other person will know what you have done, and you will signal your intention to remain aggressive.

CLAMMY HANDS

Have you ever shaken someone's hand and it was so clammy, you wanted to dry off your hand afterward? We do not like wet handshakes. We associate sweaty hands with fear. When we shake someone's sweaty palms, we may wonder what that person is afraid of, what is he hiding? The hands are the only part of the body that perspires solely in response to stress. The rest of the body perspires by stress as well, but also by temperature. Put someone on the other side of the door for a blind date or getting ready on his or her wedding day, and those palms will be dripping.

One of the few empirical studies done on handshakes took place in Sweden in the 1960's. It showed that men feel that dry hands indicate you are more social. I would say that dry hands indicate you are socially secure rather than nervous and that makes it easier to interact with you. If you have a problem with clammy hands, don't forget to wipe them on your handkerchief or tissue before you shake hands. As we've already mentioned, carry any iced drinks in your left hand at social functions, so your right will not be cold and damp when a handshake is called for.

You can also try one of the magic tricks I teach people for their job interviews. As you go in for the handshake, dry your sweaty palm off on your pants or skirt as you brush by. If sweaty palms are a regular problem for you, there is also a special palm antiperspirant for golfers and other sports enthusiasts who need a dry grip that will literally keep your palms from sweating.

LOOK, MA, NO HANDS

What do you do when the other person doesn't offer a hand? You know you are going to miss out on all the wonderful benefits of the handshake, and will have to deal with the awkwardness of establishing rapport without it. If it fits your personality or the situation, you could say as you extend your hand, "I would like to shake your hand." This technique, which I've taught for years, really works! If they absolutely will not offer their hand, they are sending you a message. A handshake is a sharing of information and a way of establishing power and showing respect. Say, for example, you're a sales rep and the prospect does not offer his hand. It may be an indication he wants to keep the upper hand and dismiss you easily.

I have been reading and watching the news looking for references to body language for many years. In many reports of the beginnings of negotiations, you can often predict the outcome by whether the two parties began with a handshake. For example, in one of the many peace talks between the Israelis and the Palestinians in 1999, The Globe reported, "The initial greeting was guarded and uneasy. The Israelis took their seats without shaking hands. The Palestinians seated around a long table did not stand to greet them. Then both sides started talking." How successful do you think those talks were?

I think we can see in the way he shakes hands, one of the reasons that George W. Bush rose to prominence. While observing his greeting behavior during his first presidential campaign, I noticed that he kept his legs slightly apart, leaned his upper body in when shaking hands, and would habitually touch people on the shoulder or the elbow and linger there. Because of the extended eye contact, softness of the touch and the lingering, his greeting was softer, warmer and more intimate than a traditional politician's handclasp.

In addition to the handshake

In addition to the effective handshake guidelines listed earlier, be sure to step forward and smile when introducing yourself or being introduced. Say your name, and repeat your newfound acquaintance's name. Then conclude with an enthusiastic pleasantry, such as, "Very good to meet you, Mr. Wesson!"

On meeting a business associate who is also a good friend or one whom you haven't seen in a long while, shake hands with them warmly. You can even use your other hand to hold their handshaking hand to show affection. If you are a man, perhaps you've done this with one of your good buddies: You see your friend, you want to hug him, but it's a business setting, so you shake hands, but that's not enough so with your free left hand in a sort of half-hug, you lean around them and hit him several times on the back. This action says symbolically, "I would love to hug you, buddy, but people are watching, so I will hit you to show how much I care." This playful "hitting not hugging" is perfectly acceptable between men in a business setting.

A Kiss Is Just a Kiss

Formal rules in American business etiquette dictate that male and female associates never kiss in public. But some industries and business, such as the entertainment industry and the arts, find it a natural part of their business culture. We generally confine those kisses to a peck on the cheek. If you don't want a big hug or kiss from someone, have your hand ready to stick out for a handshake. That will show you're not unfriendly, just a little more reserved.

Explore

1. As you walk toward someone from a distance to shake hands, notice their eyebrow flash (a quick raising of the eyebrows). The flash signals acknowledgement and precedes the handshake.
2. Observe who puts out their hand first, and who lets go first and how that affects your feelings toward the other person.
3. Pay attention to how people respond to your handshake.

Analyze

Who taught you to shake hands?

What is your comfort level when shaking hands with someone of the same sex? The opposite sex?

How do you think your handshake affects how people perceive you and your subsequent personal or business interactions?

Greeting Survey Results

Question 1. Rate the following nonverbal factors you use to form a first impression with 5 being the most important and 1 being the least important.

The most common responses in order of frequency were:

1. SMILE
2. Overall Demeanor
3. Eye contact

Men — Overall demeanor, Eye-contact, Smile & Handshake tied and attractiveness was last.

Women — Smile, Eye-Contact, Overall Demeanor, Handshake and Attractiveness.

Question 2. What is the biggest mistake someone can make when greeting another
person?
1. Lack of eye-contact
2. Not paying attention or appearing disinterested
Even though females chose a smile as the most important factor used in forming a first impression they felt that not making eye contact was the biggest
mistake.
The men chose not paying attention or appearing disinterested as their top
choice for biggest mistake.

Question 3. Which of the following do you generally prefer to have offered to you as
a greeting by a person you are meeting for the first time?
1. A handshake is the generally preferred greeting for initial meetings
84% of the women chose Handshake
98% of the men chose Handshake

Question 4a. Do you like to shake hands?
1. 88% of participants answered "yes"; they like to shake hands
85% of the women answered "yes"
96% of the men answered "yes"

Question 4b. Of the people that answered yes,
1. 23% said they liked a handshake because it established a connection. (Even
scores between men and women)
2. Allows me to make physical contact
3. Helps me learn about another person.
4. Helps me learn what the person thinks about me

Question 5. How would you describe the way you shake hands
76% of the sample described their handshake as "firm" (some alternative
phrases used were strong, solid) 81% of the men and 73% of the women
12% of the 76% went further to describe their handshake as firm with eye-
contact and a smile
11% of the 72% went further to describe their handshake as quick with one
shake

Question 6. How does shaking hands with someone affect your interaction?
44% felt it helped them get an impression of the other person so they can go
into the interaction prepared. 51% of the men and 41% of the women
38% felt it helps to build a connection, and/or increase comfort level and/or
build mutual respect. 29% of the men and 42% of the women (notice women's
numbers — perhaps if with a man in business this would make a difference —
do men not shake hands with women)

Question 7a. Do you think someone's handshake can tell you something about him or
her?
93% responded YES
92 % of the women and 98 % of the men

Question 7b. If yes, what do you think someone's handshake tells you about him/her?
The most common answers (in descending order of frequency) were:
1. Confidence: The top response with 40%: self-confidence and confidence in meeting others, if someone is comfortable with him/herself. Firm/strong handshake = confident, self-assured. Weak handshake = not confident/insecure
2. Personality/character: whether the person is outgoing/introverted, friendliness, if the person has a strong or weak personality. Weak & limp handshake = weak personality, shy
3. Control/authority/power: Firm handshake = in control, weak handshake = passivity
4. Superiority: handshake that's too firm indicates overcompensating, egomania, letting you know they're strong.

Question 8. What is the number one mistake a person can make when shaking hands with someone?
1. 41% of total said to limp, 34% of the women and 53% of the men
2. 18% mentioned eye contact
3. 12% said "too hard"
4. Disinterested/not fully present
5. Sweaty palms

Question 9a. Have you ever been in a situation where you wanted to shake hands and did not have the opportunity?
67% said yes, 66% of the females and 69% of the men

Question 9b. If yes, how did you feel?
Men's responses: slower to establish a connection, feeling left out, not given respect, like a stranger, no connection
Women's responses: Rejected, left out, insignificant, missed an opportunity to make a good first impression, feeling of not fitting in, didn't fit in, negative feelings towards those that snubbed, not able to make a connection.

Question 9c. If you do not have the opportunity to shake hands, do you think it takes longer to feel comfortable with others?
51% responded yes, 52% of the women and 51% of the men (no real difference)

Question 10. If a person did not shake hands with you even though you extended your hand, what would you think about that person?
1. Rude, untrustworthy and unfriendly and not interested in the person offering hands at 93% of the responses.
2. Only 7% considered it might be unintentional and would not be affected.
2/3 of the 7% were female, showing that females might be more likely to take it less personally.

Question 11. What would keep you from shaking hands with someone? (Social vs. business)
Dirty hands, germs, or illness as their reason. 61% of the females and 48% of the males. (SO are men not as aware of germs or feel they must despite germs.

General feel of survey is that there is less of a social expectation for females to shake hands — new question)
Take the cue from the other person. 18% of the women and 7% of the men.

Question 12a. Would your decision to buy from someone be influenced by the type of handshake he/she gave you?
1. 50% yes and 50% no

Question 12b. If yes, what kind of handshake would make you not buy from someone?
1. No palm-to-palm contact defined as a grip at the ends of your fingers or arching the palm
2. Palms touch but little or no pressure
3. Bone crushed
Little pressure tied with 34% each
- 39% of the women chose little pressure
- 32% of the men chose bone crusher

Question 13. How does the gender of the person you're shaking hands with affect your handshake?
1. Gender does not matter. 65% of the women said the gender did not matter while 55% of the men change the way they shake hands depending on gender. Most men would use a gentler handshake with a woman and a firmer grip with another man.

Question 14. Are you more comfortable shaking hands with a man or a woman?
1. 78% surveyed are more comfortable shaking hands with a man.
2. 79% of the women were more comfortable shaking a man's hand
3. 82% of the men were more comfortable shaking hands with a man.

Question 14. Rate your concern about getting germs from handshakes from 1 to 5 with 1 being not concerned at all and 5 being extremely concerned.
1. 41% of those that responded were not concerned at all. 33% of the males and 45% of the females.
2. Only 6% responded extremely concerned, 8% of the women and 4% of the men
3. Another 7% rated this 4 (Concerned), 10% of the women and 2% of the men.

Of note here is that of the people who chose a 1 (not concerned at all), 35% of them noted in question 11 that dirty hands, illness would stop them from shaking hands. 53% of those who chose 3 slightly concerned did the same thing.

Chapter 7

Space and Territory

TO MOST PEOPLE, KATHRYN WOULD SEEM TO BE A CONTRADICTION in body language. She is vivacious and friendly, is involved in community activities (they call her Ms. Volunteer) and loves to talk. Actually, talking is what she does best. When you go to lunch with her, it seems that she can have a conversation about anything. She is a really fun person and people who know her love her dearly. Yet you should never mistake her involvement, friendliness and ability to talk to mean she wants you to hug her, touch her, or even stand close to her.

People who don't know Kathryn well make that misjudgment all the time. Someone will be standing next to Kathryn as she tells a story and unconsciously step in close. Kathryn will physically pull away when people do that. Or someone might walk up to her and stand a foot and half away and she will automatically step back to give herself half a foot more space. And if a person tries to step in really close to hug her as they greet her or say goodbye, she will pull her head back and her arch her upper body away. Katherine is definitely not a "close talker." With these behaviors, Kathryn is letting others know she needs a lot of space, and indicating exactly where her personal space boundaries begin and end.

We all have spatial boundary zones that vary from inches to feet depending on the situation, the topic and who we are speaking with. Some people like to stand close to others and some like to stand far apart. Some people enjoy spreading out into larger territories, while others are comfortable in smaller spaces. The amount of space that you choose for your body bubble will affect your interactions.

Analyze

You are waiting alone for an elevator and a stranger walks down the hall, comes beside you and stands less than a foot away facing the elevator doors. How do you feel? You step on the elevator and turn to face back towards the door and the stranger steps facing toward you less than a foot from your face. How do you feel?

What is our comfort zone?

The comfort zone is the zone of space we like to have around us for certain types of interactions. In 1959, anthropologist Edward Hall discovered that though we don't talk about it and can't see it, we respect certain invisible walls of space. He conducted numerous studies and found that people in the U.S. had four distinct comfort distances, each with their own specific ranges of comfort, and that these distances were surprisingly universal to most Americans. He also noted that comfort zones varied drastically between cultures. Knowing the standard zones that other people keep can help you know whether someone wants to do business with you, respects you, or wants to have your child. Let's look at the different kinds of zones we all have.

The Intimate Zone is generally between six and eighteen inches. We reserve this space for friends and family. It's what I call "kissy face" distance. We allow others to encroach on this zone in a few other situations: contact sports and dancing and in greeting and goodbyes. In North American culture this space is almost like an extension of your body. Standing 18 inches from someone, you can only see the face, upper body and hands, while the feet are out of vision range. If you get closer than 18 inches, everything blurs. This makes you vulnerable to attack. At this distance you will be able to smell and touch the other person and they can smell and touch you, so you want to make sure you have used your deodorant and brushed your teeth. This distance is used for sexual contact or comforting someone. Our intimate body bubble is bigger in front than it is in back and smaller around our feet, so people can stand closer to us when they are behind us. Think of queuing for lines and elevator spacing.

Beyond that is the Personal Zone, your personal body space of 1 to 4 feet. This is the social gathering distance we reserve for people who are friendly. I call this the "martini" distance.

From four to 12 feet is the Social Zone. I call this the "stranger introduction distance." We hold this distance between ourselves and the express delivery guy, a new neighbor, or team members at work. The handshake shrinks this distance back down to the intimate zone. We like to maintain this distance in formal interactions such as business meetings or interviews. There is a wonderful story about how people who were meeting President Kennedy for the first time would approach and then stop around ten feet away. People who worked in the White House saw this happen over and over again until they began to call ten feet, "presidential space."

The Public Distance zone is 12 feet to the line of sight. This is reserved for such things as public speaking and lectures, plays and concerts and sporting events. I was talking to Chris, a collegian who regularly attended US Open tennis matches. He had gone for years to an old arena which was small and where every seat gave you a great view of the players. When the Open moved to another venue, the new venue featured reserved seats closer to the action, but these were for corporate sponsors. You had to pay $100 for the nosebleed seats, where he said all you could see were dots on the courts. He had chosen on this particular trip to buy cheap passes that allowed him to walk around and watch the players warming up by standing close to practice courts. The passes also allowed him to watch the early rounds or the tournament up close in the old stadium nearby. He said, "I like to see their faces when they're playing well and hitting the ball 'smack on.' It's the best."

Why is understanding space important?

The study of space (called proxemics) gives a lot of nonverbal information about the level of trust and intimacy that people have for you. You can read people's level of comfort with you by noticing the amount of distance they keep between themselves and you. Understanding proxemics can also prevent you from unknowingly violating personal space and causing someone tension or getting a black eye.

The well-known communications expert Alfred Mehrabian found that "People are drawn toward persons and things they like, evaluate highly, and prefer; they avoid or move away from things they dislike, evaluate negatively, or do not prefer." I'm sure this seems pretty obvious to most of us. But what we don't realize is that this psychological attraction and avoidance of things and people we like and dislike also shows itself in how we move physically. And by noticing the dance of space in various kinds of interactions you can understand yourself and other people.

Closer and farther away

As you interact with others, you actually move closer or farther away depending on your feelings about the other person. Sometimes this is expressed in what we call an "abbreviated form of approach" — stepping or leaning toward or away from a person. The more cues we give, the more the parts of our body pull, lean or arch toward or away, the more interest or disinterest we will show. You would naturally lean toward a speaker who is talking about something you like and are therefore interested in, no matter how close or far away the speaker is to you. When attending a meeting, you will sit down next to people you like and agree with about the topic for the meeting, but you'll put a distance between yourself and someone you dislike. When people ask me to analyze the body language of movie star couples in photographs, one of the first things I look at and measure is the space between the bodies, and whether their bodies are close or apart.

Watch people at an office party and notice the nonverbal mingling behavior. Those who are friendly and familiar will gather in close clusters, sitting or standing. People we think of as warm will greet people as they come into the room by moving toward them and touching them with either a handshake, a pat on the back, a touch on the arm or shoulder, most of these from a foot and half away. Or, they might even go into the intimate zone for a hug or a kiss.

When you are in a group and you stand further away from the others, some people in the group might see you as aloof. You will seem more open if you stand at the closer edge of the appropriate distance for the relationship, which is 14 to 24 inches from a friend and no more than four feet from someone you've just met.

Why is getting into someone's space so threatening?

The territorial space that people claim as distinctly belonging to them is their intimate space, 0 to 18 inches. When someone gets inside that space and we don't know them or don't trust them, it feels at a primal level as if they are there to attack. The area less than 18 inches from you is reserved for kissing and other contact sports, so anyone else in that space is assumed to be attacking. We will instinctively move away from the person to put them outside attack range.

I used to teach an interrogation technique to police officers using this information. When officers deliberately invade the personal space of their suspect during an interview, they can read the cues of the suspect to gauge their innocence or guilt. It's also something they can use as an intimidation technique.

What is our territory?

Your primary territory consists of places or locations you have occupied for what you consider a significant period of time: your house, your place at the family dinner table. You have exclusive control over primary territories like your toothbrush, your pillow, your favorite pen, your Barcalounger, or the parking space with your name on it.

Areas we do not own but with which you are associated are your "secondary territory." They include your office chair, your seat in a meeting, your seat on the subway, your stool at the local bar, your pew in church or the coffee cup you always claim in the break room. When you are sitting at a restaurant, your silverware, glasses and cup mark the boundaries of your secondary territory. Markers help others know that for now this secondary territory is yours.

I have a friend Jeff who is a humorous speaker. In one of his routines, he jokes about the tall guy that always sits in front of you in the movie theater. He tells the audience that the best way to prevent this is to claim the seats in front you by covering them with Popcorn. The pop corn becomes a clear and very messy marker. Of course, Jeff's mother is still telling him she did not raise him to leave popcorn in a seat!

I was sitting at my desk in the outer office on the day of major layoffs. Sixty rather high-level employees were let go. Each was escorted back to his/her desk. I am sure they considered those desks their primary territory. But the office considered them only secondary territory. They were given a little cardboard boxes in which to put what the company considered their primary territory items in to take home. The guard watched to make sure no company property was taken. The former employees were allowed to take their photographs and framed degrees and certificates and candy. I saw them come out again, heads bowed and silent, carrying their little boxes. Losing their jobs was a horrible experience and they had the added humiliation of losing their desks and carrying out their belongings in a box. Tip: We have attachments to our space, even seemingly business secondary territory spaces that we should respect and honor. Instead of walking right into someone's cubicle, approach slowly, stand at the invisible outer wall and knock on the cubicle wall to ask for entry. If you need a stapler, ask before you borrow it. What is one man's public territory is another's primary territory.

You share public territory like parks, sidewalks, and restaurants. In public territories, you see people claim the space temporarily by leaving a marker like a book at a library table, a folded newspaper at a coffee house table, a blanket on a park lawn. So how do you sum this up? Well you might stand twelve inches from your sweetie, four feet from your boss and eight feet from a movie star.

What happens when someone invades your territory?

If someone invades your territory, you will generally choose one of three options. You will leave, you will put up boundaries or you will defend yourself. Interestingly enough, in our normal day-to-day interactions we rarely fight anybody that comes into our personal space and territory. We tend to go with the flow. My friend Sue has a big two-story house and a husband who travels three weeks out of the month. That means the house pretty much belongs to her and her daughter.

She called me one night, angry with her husband. "He comes home from a trip and leaves a trail of his stuff throughout the house. His shoes are on the coffee table, his sweater is on the bar stool, his briefcase and computer are on the kitchen table and his baseball cap is on top of the toaster oven! I feel like I have been invaded by Huns!"

Sue didn't yell at her jet-lagged husband, which was wise. I told her that he was just establishing the house as his again by leaving his marks everywhere. She said he needed to be a little less invasive.

(Funny thing was that I used to room with Sue. She was working 12 hours a day on a movie set, so I did all the house cleaning. The house felt like mine. She would come home, leave her shoes on the couch, her papers on the dining room table and her sweater on the kitchen bar. I would swoop up all her things and put them in her room in an attempt to clean. She would get mad, saying, "It's my house, too!" It made perfect sense that she needed to leave the markers to make the house hers.)

Exercise

How do you feel as someone enters your intimate zone of space? What if it's a friend or a pet? What if it's a stranger or someone you don't get along with? Read the following scenarios and explain how you would react in each one. Ask other people you know how they would respond. You will have some lively discussions.

- You are waiting in line for a cup of coffee and someone cuts in front of you in line.
- You are not getting along with your co-worker, but you have to sit in the same cubicle with them all day.
- You are sitting at your desk and someone you don't know comes in and stands next to you.
- You are in a meeting and a co-worker picks up your pen and begins to use it.
- You get to the meeting late and someone is sitting in "your" seat.

How do I know if someone needs more space?

When any individual is threatened, their personal space expands. They want more space around them so they feel safer. People who work in a stressful office will make their cubicles "bigger" by placing their little trash cans or an extra chair just outside their cubicle walls. Look for "insulation cues." Any inanimate object that is placed between you and the person with whom you are talking is an indication of defensiveness. Setting a table, desk, pillows, drinking glass or other object between you and the other person is the unconscious equivalent of shielding your body from attack and provides you with protection from something we do not like. A person who creates barriers between himself and the other person all the time may have low self-esteem, or may be hiding something. I trained foster parents to look for nonverbal cues in their new foster children that indicated they had been abused or did not feel secure. Constantly holding toys or blankets in front of their bodies, even in seemingly safe situations, is an indication a child is afraid. The toy or blanket acts as a shield from an attack. Any child may need such comfort, but again, habitual use in safe situations is a cause for concern.

Do men and women feel differently about space and territory?

Yes. Men and women feel invasion from different perspectives.

In a study, males and females were sitting alone at tables in a university library. As they tended to their business, they were "invaded" by a male or female "invader" from either a face-to-face or an adjacent position. If the invader was face-to-face, men responded negatively and women felt no effect. If the invader sat next to them, the males felt no effect and the women responded negatively. This makes sense, as another study done by Byrne and Fisher in 1975 showed that American men generally chose to sit across from people whom they considered their friends and American women chose to sit adjacent to the people they considered to be their friends. Additionally, the study showed that men did not like strangers sitting across from them and women did not like having strangers sitting next to them.

Men tend to get more aggressive and women are more likely to give way, but most on both sides go with the flow. What is really interesting is how gender affects what we consider invasion. Consider the following study.

This second study also took place in a library and confirmed that both genders use territorial markers to protect the space they see as threatened. Males erected barriers between themselves and facing positions and females erected barriers between themselves and adjacent positions. There is also an interesting study about armrests on airplanes done a few years ago. When women took the middle armrest, men over 40 fought to claim it as their own and men under 40 gave the armrests to the women, no matter what age the woman. I was talking about this to a client of mine, who has a high-level position in her company. She travels internationally almost every other week. She said the first thing she does when she gets on the plane is plant her arm on the middle armrest. She doesn't take it down till she is sure the guy sitting next to her is clear that the armrest is hers!

Men getting on an elevator will tend to stand closer to those who do not make eye contact with them. Females do the same when the person or people are male. However, if a female makes contact with another female by smiling at her, it is perceived as invading space. The woman's eye contact and smiling seems to say, "Come stand next to me. Let's talk."

Are space and the invasion of it perceived differently across cultures?

It is so different it would require a separate book to describe. So instead, I will give you a few examples to give you an idea of the extreme difference. You're an American visiting St. Petersburg in Russia. Russians lean over you in the bakery, shove to get a better place in line and think nothing of touching your arm as they jostle for space. For many of us, this behavior would lead to a fight. One professor who lived in St Petersburg said, "A few days of such 'molestation' by dozens of Russian strangers can scramble the nerves of all but the most traveled foreign visitor."

Normally, you might leave a space of a foot and half between you and the next person in line and not look over their shoulder. A Russian entering would see all that space and assume you are not in line. He or she would get between you and the person in front of you, leaving less than two inches between them and the person in front. If you don't move to within two inches of him, somebody else will come and step in front of you again! Russians' personal distance is only a few inches, which is the space that we in North America reserve for "kissy face" and attack. Russians don't want to kiss or hit us, they just don't understand our need for space.

I was giving a public speaking training class for a Japanese-owned company. When we began to discuss some of the cultural differences in public speaking, an amazing story came out. The big boss came over from Japan to give a speech. Near the end of his speech, he called the Japanese manager of the American-based plant to the front of the auditorium. He proceeded to yell and scream at him for his ineptitude, taking a piece of paper and hitting him on top of the head with it. The boss was invading the manager's space both aurally and physically. The employee stood and continued taking the punishment, bowing lower and lower as it became more intense, showing his shame and respect for the big boss's power until he was literally kicked out of the room, (yes physically kicked) and banished back to Japan. Not only was the manager physically attacked and his space invaded, but his level of power in that culture left him with no alternative but to submit and leave the territory of the plant he had been in charge of just an hour previously. My friend, who was the plant manager at the time, wound up quitting. He said he couldn't keep his American employees. Of course, they would have been highly uncomfortable with that sort of "space invasion."

My friend Michael, who lives in Paris recently wrote about space issues on his blog.

"One thing I love and hate in France is the closeness of personal space — personal spaces being the invisible barrier people have around them to protect their intimacy. In France, the distance between two people talking can be much closer than in the U.S. I have actually done a table dance with a colleague while having coffee together as he continually moved around the table, closer to me, as we were discussing an issue.

Now, I know it wasn't because he was attracted to me! I've observed the same behavior from him with other people. And it's not just him that I've watched have this similar type of behavior. People in France simply have a smaller personal space than in other countries..."

So where should I sit?

That depends upon what you want to do with the other person. When you cancel gender differences, it's generally best to sit side-by-side because it fosters cooperation. By sitting by someone's side, we enhance cooperative behavior from them by conveying that we are not competing against them. It also insures that both of you are facing in the direction of the problem or project, such as a report on the table or research material that needs organizing. Imagine men lined up to go into battle. They are side-to-side and shoulder-to-shoulder, facing a common foe.

Opposite sides foster competition. Sitting directly across from someone, such as an employer sitting direct across from a prospective applicant with a table in between them, tends to foster a competitive attitude.

Sit at a 90-degree angle for good conversation. The best seating position at a table for a cooperative exchange of information is at the corner of the table. One person takes one side of the corner and the other person takes the other side. The benefits of this position are (1) it allows both parties to enter into each other's personal space, creating a stronger bond than if they remained distant from each other and (2) it breaks up the stuffy formality of the situation by moving you closer to others. The corner of the table adds a bit of psychological security for both parties by having a bit of a barrier between them, but it is not as much of a barrier as if you sat opposite one another.

The overall goal is to sit as close as you can to the other person without making them feel uncomfortable. This will create the most intimate communication.

What can space tell us about power?

I was standing outside the Mirage Hotel in Las Vegas with my fellow conventioneers when I turned and saw Kevin Costner come out of the door. I froze, awestruck, wanting to go closer but respecting the space given as a privilege of his charismatic star power. The two big security guys flanking him were also a deterrent!

Space tells us who is important and who has privilege. Space can also tell us a lot about the status, confidence, and the power of the people around us. Just look at your own workplace and examine who has the biggest office or the biggest cubicle space. Walk down a hallway and see who does not give way to discover who has the most power. Power also gives you privacy. The big guns might have their own corner office apart from the plebes scrunched together in cubicles. I recently had a phone conversation with someone interested in hiring a professional colleague of mine. She described with great anxiety how the overcrowding in the office would force my colleague to be in an open space with other employees' desks right next to his and that students could easily come up and talk with him. She said, "He is so overqualified for this job that I am concerned that offering this space would be an insult to him and the working conditions would be too stressful for someone in such a high position." In other words, the space did not fit his power position. I assured her my friend would not be ruffled. I found out that she had asked the same thing of my friend's other references. They too assured her that his power parameters were not going to be affected in the least. He got the job, but he almost didn't get it because of the link between office space and power.

Confident people and people of higher status are comfortable going straight to the center of the attention while lower status or non-confident people tend to hover near the exits or the back of the room. University studies have shown that the students who choose to sit front and center in the classroom received the highest grades in the class, while those who sat in the back and at the corners of the room received the worst grades. Confident students choose center front seats and are rewarded with the teachers more personal attention which in turn affects their learning and grades.

The size and dynamics of your territory also change your power

When I was teaching at Florida State and working on my doctorate, I had the opportunity to work with the dean of the College of Communication, Dr. Ted Clevenger. Dr. Clevenger was an incredibly smart man but also an incredibly kind man. On my list of people I have most admired in my life, he is in the top five. Unfortunately, because he was so empathetic and understanding, both students and faculty began to think of him as a soft touch and he lost some of his power. I don't know how he found out about it. But I know he was a man of great integrity and he wasn't about to be anything other than the man he was. He couldn't change his character, but he could change his territory. So he did what very few people think of doing to change their reputations. He redecorated. Dr. Clevenger's old office had a small desk with a small chair for him and an equally small chair on the visitor's side of the desk. The colors and style of the walls and accoutrements were bland and institutional.

Small, bland and institutional were not words that you would use to describe his new office. The walls were golden yellow. An oriental rug covered most of the gray carpeting, but it was the furniture that really created a dramatic impact. The little metal desk was replaced with a large mahogany desk. The wood was dark and the size imposing. His little chair was exchanged for a large high-backed red leather chair, the kind a king or at least the head of large corporation would sit in. On either side, slightly behind the desk and chair were large palm trees, the kind you would find in a jungle on either side of a lounging lion. There was one piece of furniture that remained from his old office: the small visitor chair, although I think they sawed off part of the legs to make it even smaller

Guess what happened? His reputation changed. Nobody saw him as a pushover anymore. He was King of the Jungle. Not surprising, as soon as he sat in his red throne chair, he held his head higher, the chin slightly above the "center line." He didn't rest his arms together on the desk as he used to, but stretched them out wide on the throne's leather chair arms. His shoulders were held just slightly back as if he were about to hold court. Even his voice had changed. It still had his energy, but rather than being tentative, it was just a little more imperious and sure. People changed their response to him as well. Students and teachers alike, who used to walk casually into to his office, stood at the open door and knocked gently on the doorframe awaiting permission to cross the threshold. Now, as they sat in the little metal chair looking up at Dean Clevenger, their voices became tentative and their body language not quite as cocky. It worked for him. He was still one of the kindest men I have ever known, but people did not take advantage of him and all was right in the kingdom.

How should you seat groups of people?

It depends on what activity you want to encourage. If you want people to visit, share ideas, bond and create agreement, put them in "social seating." This spacing actually brings people together, like team style seating in a classroom or the dining table in most homes. The people are facing each other around a table but the table breadth is no more than three feet, so they are still in personal distance. If you want them to be quiet, be obedient and listen, use sociofugal seating. This creates spacing which separates people so no one faces anyone else. We see this in the straight rows of chairs found in airports or bus terminals.

Positions at a table also communicate power. In Western cultures, a father traditionally sits at the head of the table facing the other members of the family, appropriate to his primary role in patriarchal societies.

Is seating the same across cultures?

Each culture organizes space differently depending on what kind of interaction they value. For example, in North American corporate offices, the boss is usually on the highest floor in a private corner office. It's hard for people to get to him and they may even have to go through other people like secretaries. As you might guess, this means he or she doesn't get much personal contact with ordinary workers.

In France, the offices are set up so the boss is in the center office. They still are a little hard to get to, but the protection comes from the layers of lesser-powered workers radiating out from their central power position, sort of like a queen bee surrounded by drones. In contrast, Japanese offices are commonly set up with the boss's desk at the end of a row of pushed together desks that subordinate employees use. That's right, the boss is right there looking over your desk. He or she does not have privacy and that maximizes his interaction with his workers.

My friend John used to work as a plant manager for a Japanese-owned company here in the United States. He told me that Japanese company policy was to build cubicle walls where the partitions were low enough to see the tops of the Japanese employees' heads. When he asked why he had to make this costly change, he was told it was so the boss could look out and see if everyone was working. Privacy was not allowed.

Does space affect the emotional impact of a message?

Yes indeedy. It's one of the most forceful ways to communicate. Proxemics can be used in combination with other behaviors to add emphasis to the message. For example, if a boss is angry with you and invades your intimate space, then the perceived threat of anger is higher than if he were angry with you but stayed on the other side of the room. If you're a woman and a man stares at you from across the room, invading your visual space, there is less threat than if he is sitting at the table right next to you.

Does the amount of space we keep from others change as our relationship with them changes?

Well, it does, but there is a gender exception. Guys maintain the same distance with their friends as they do with their colleagues. Women get closer physically with other women the closer they feel emotionally. In 1972, two researchers, Heshka and Nelson, secretly photographed pairs of adults as they walked down the street, and gauged the distance between them. After taking the photograph, the researcher approached the unknowing participants and asked what type of relationship they had. They discovered that female/female pairs interacted at closer distances as their relationship became closer, while distance between male/male pairs did not change as the friendship changed.

Explore

Expand your body bubble of space. Put more distance between yourself and the people you are normally close to. Describe what happens. Now, reduce your zone of space. Put less distance between yourself and strangers. Get inside their bubbles. Stand close to people on elevators. Sit down at a restaurant table with a stranger and watch out! Things can get interesting. Choose someone small and unarmed. Describe what happens.

Here are some findings from participants of body language training workshops participants who did the above exercise:

"I am a 'touchy feely' person with close relatives and close friends. So I decided to observe behavior regarding 'bubble space' with someone who really knows me. It had been about two weeks since the last time I saw my first cousin, Nina. I called her up and we met for lunch at our local restaurant. When we approached each other, I rubbed my cheek with her cheek instead of my usual hug and kiss. Immediately, my cousin asked if there was something wrong. I replied with 'What do you mean? I'm fine.' After we checked in with the restaurant hostess, we sat down in the lobby on a long sofa bench. Nina sat down first and then I sat down a little further away from her than usual. The space between us could have easily seated another person. She first looked at me and inquired again with 'Do you want to tell me about it?' I said 'What do you mean, talk about what?' After I finally convinced her I was fine, she then wanted to know if she had done something to hurt me. What I found out in this observation is that my cousin did not attempt to invade my space. She remained in her own space."

— June Thompkins

"This happened to me at Oglethorpe College near Atlanta last semester. On the second night of class, I sat down in a desk only to have a classmate come in later and stand over me just giving me 'that look' which I immediately recognized as saying I was in 'her' chair. There were no markers (for assigned seats) and we were so early into the semester that one would not assume chairs to have already been claimed. I smiled and said, 'Would you like to have this chair?' She replied, 'Yes, I am somewhat of a creature of habit.' I moved to another chair. I might add that this is a person I like and had been in class with before."

— Betty McKee

"When Lori and I sit down to talk or watch TV, we usually sit very close together. Usually I put my arm around her or we hold hands. Sunday night her parents were putting in new carpeting and moving furniture from room to room. To get some privacy, we went downstairs to an empty room. I sat down against the wall, and she asked me to sit with her. I told her that my back was bothering me and that I was more comfortable leaning against the wall. She then pulled the bag against the wall. When I did not move, she asked me in her whiney voice to sit with her. I did, with my hands behind my head, leaning against the wall. She then asked me, 'What is wrong?' I said, 'Nothing, I'm just very tired.' Suddenly she grabbed my hand, put it around her shoulders and whined, 'I want you to hold me,' She continued to hold my hand on her shoulder as we talked."

— John Shaber

"I decided to perform my experiment at two parties that I had attended. I chose to manipulate space during introductions. Since I attended these parties as the guest of an invited person, I knew that I would make many new acquaintances. I didn't want to perform this exercise on my friends or family members because I thought our relationships would affect the results. To clarify, I considered your suggestion to keep out of the zone of space with someone that you are normally very close to, but assumed its results would consist of responses independent of space manipulation. My doubt: would someone usually intimate with me be solely affected by my sudden distance? Or would their response also result from their concern for my welfare? I realized that strangers would offer a nonbiased reaction.

I utilized an exaggerated distance on the first night and a noticeable lack of distance on the second night. In further explanation, I shook hands from the distance of a locked arm while bending slightly back in contrast to stepping toe-to-toe during handshakes. Both of these stances differ from the space normally experienced. Despite my initial skepticism, I received reactions startling in their similarities; these reactions appeared consistently in differing age groups, genders, and ethnicities.

Uniformly, persons stepped forward or leaned inward when I greeted them from a distance. I surmise that they felt that I was 'dodging' them. Also, three of approximately twelve people asked my date if I was shy. I noticed that most persons raised their heads during our introductions. Was this a sign of dominance? Why? I spoke in a pleasant tone and quite freely, meaning I wasn't overly quiet. I maintained my vocal tone and amount of discourse on the following night. I again perceived a sign from the placement of the persons' heads.

When I stepped abnormally close during introductions, people usually lowered their heads with a sideward glance. This action occurred in greetings where the other person stood taller than me. I found that really surprising. Was it a sign of submission? Why? I wasn't loud or vocally aggressive. Although not everyone looked away, they all stepped back. Had I 'attacked' them? I believe that it made them uncomfortable because of the way they reacted.

I enjoyed this exercise since I never truly recognized the existence of assumed space. I learned how people consider it an important possession. However, I fear that I may have abused the exercise. I wonder about those persons' first impressions of me."

— Carl Shepherd

Chapter 8

Body Windows and the Upper Torso, Lower Torso, and Feet

WE HAVE "WINDOWS" ALL OVER OUR BODIES: AT THE TOP OF OUR head, our eyes, our mouth, our throat, our upper chest or heart, the palms of our hands, our knees, and at the bottoms of our feet. I began to name these parts of the body "windows" when I noticed in my nonverbal communication course at Florida State that my students, all 150 of them in one class, would open their windows when the information in class was compelling and they were fully present. And indeed, your body windows open and close depending on how we are feeling about ourselves, the topic, or the situation. When we like someone, we want to have our bodies open to that person. For instance when you're seated at a bar, you will look at and turn toward someone who interests you and turn and look away from someone you are not interested in.

When I was little, I would sit in the grass in the back yard and play with roly-poly bugs. If I touched one, it would roll up in a tight little ball to protect itself. Likewise, we roll our bodies inward or take other actions to protect ourselves from people we do not like or feel safe with. We may bring our shoulders inward, cross our arms, zip up a jacket, or put on a pair of sunglasses. When we are nervous, we also close our body windows. We may cross our legs, arms or ankles, hide the palms of our hands, bring our heads down or close our eyes momentarily by blinking. Physical barriers and objects also offer us a way to close our windows by closing us off from others. Women may hold a purse in front of their bodies; girls may place their school books in front of their chests, Men may put on a tie or hold a drink at chest level. In business we put a desk between ourselves and the salesperson whose product does not interest us; we will put a counter or a glass window between ourselves and a pesky customer.

Our body windows signal to others whether we are open or closed. When we are speaking to someone with whom we feel familiar and comfortable, we may open our heart window and face him or her directly. We often unfold our arms, signaling to others that we are open to approach. Our arm cross can also signal openness. If we have our arms uncrossed and our hands relaxed at our sides, we can send the message: I am open to approach. If we cross our arms tightly, we may send the message: I am closed to approach.

In photos of Nicole Kidman and Tom Cruise in the last few years of their relationship, Nicole was often photographed with her body turned away from Tom and her arms crossed in front of her chest or arms and hands over her lower torso. I analyzed hundred of these photos for the media. The symbolic message was powerful. Her hands provided a barrier to particular parts of her body. She was symbolically closing herself off sexually from him. The public image projected was: he is not my sexual partner.

Often this unusual posture indicates that someone feels she have been either physically or emotionally injured by her partner. It's a common pose by women whose husbands have been unfaithful or when wives no longer want to have sex with their partners. She stopped posing this way until she started dating again. And now the hands are higher and the clasp is often tense as it in the promotional photo for the film, The Interpreter where she is often shown symbolically holding her own hand, closing the window at the palm of the hand. This pose showed that Nicole wanted to comfort herself when out in public.

Openness is allowing people to make contact with you and the willingness to make contact with them. However, you may appear too familiar if you get too close and open too much of your body to someone with whom you do not have a close relationship or a stranger who doesn't respond to your approach by opening up in kind. A woman can appear overly familiar if she opens up her heart window too much by wearing a low cut sweater, or overly aloof by wearing a turtle neck or a frilly buttoned-at-the-neck blouse with a floppy bow tied in a knot.

Liars tend to close entrances to hide the truth. To spot a liar, notice if the person turns away the head or heart or covers the window at the mouth.

Of course I would be remiss if I didn't mention that just like the windows on a house, the opening and closing of body windows are affected by environmental factors such as temperature. Think about what happens to your body when you are physically cold. Your muscles tighten and you hold your arms tight to your chest and the fingers of your hands tight and close together. When you are warm, your muscles relax. When you go to sit down, you sit back in your chair, your legs stretch out and let go, your fingers open out. It's interesting that the same body language in response to temperature symbolically shows us as cold or warm emotionally.

THE HEART WINDOW

The central window is the heart window. It is an indicator of someone's emotional state. It is a key indicator of how we feel about ourselves and others around us. The heart window of a person's body is on the upper middle of the chest right where the heart is.

Exercise: As you're reading this, place the palm of your hands on that part of your chest right now. Leave them there for a minute. Now take them down. Do you feel a little more vulnerable?

To understand the concept of heart windows, imagine that you protect this window as a knight's armor or an umpire's chest pad protects his or her chest. Now, think beyond that to something more abstract, and imagine that your window opens to the innermost part of you — your spirit, your secrets, all your dreams and fears. Thus, to have your window open to another, you make yourself more vulnerable. In general, an open window indicates a friendly, positive attitude toward a person. A closed heart window shows a desire to protect yourself or close yourself off from someone or something you do not like or want to be exposed to.

We open and close our heart window in four ways: through the clothing we wear, the way we position our heart window towards or away from someone, the use of physical barriers like books and counters, and finally, through our arm and shoulder placement.

I believe that the heart window is one of the most significant parts of the body to examine to reveal the secrets of someone's true feelings. In order to understand the significance of the heart window, let's look at how we use some of the barriers to close it.

Quite obviously clothing shows whether a window is open or closed. Imagine the difference between a woman in a low cut sweater or a high neck blouse. Imagine John Travolta's character in the classic disco movie Saturday Night Fever wearing a buttoned-up oxford shirt instead of the open-to-the-waist shirt that bares his gold-chained chest. Can you see the President come out for the State of the Union address wearing a tank top? Hiding or revealing the heart window with low or high neck clothing creates an impression of a person as loose or tight, reserved or wild.

Did you ever wonder why men wear an incredibly expensive piece of cloth tied around their necks in a knot? From an objective standpoint, it seems ridiculous. But a tie is a designer curtain covering up the heart window. The tie is only worn in formal work or social situations to indicate the seriousness of the business at hand and show the status of the wearer. What do men do when they leave work and go home or go out with friends? They loosen up or take off their ties, opening their heart and throat windows.

The reason men wear something so uncomfortable is that it's a symbol of business formality. In fact, in the early 1980s when women were making in-roads into more equal positions in the workplace, they began to wear big, wide bows around the necks of their blouses. Then in the mid-80s, they wore big scarves that covered their heart. They needed to show they were serious about taking on the workplace and needed the protection of the bows and scarves to cover up their heart windows like a knight's armor. It physically and symbolically also covered up and protected their sexuality.

We not only use clothing to open or close the heart window but also body movement. When we face toward someone, we have our heart window open. When we turn the body away from them and present the side, then we close off the heart window and effectively protect the heart. In college I took a fencing course, I wanted to be a female Errol Flynn and use my foil "beat six, lock and parry four" with the bad guys and swing from chandeliers. One of the basic principals in fencing is to stand sideways with only the shoulder of your foil hand facing towards your opponent. If any of your heart window showed, you presented a target for the foil. I spent a spent a semester nursing big bruises on my chest till I learned the value of protecting the heart window.

Exercise

The next time you go to shake hands, try shaking hands with someone with your shoulder, rather than your front, pointing at the person. Then shake hands with that same person or someone else face- to- face — that is, with heart windows vulnerable. Compare the first interaction with the second.

UPPER BODY SIGNALS — SHOULDERS AND ARMS

The upper body or torso includes shoulders, arms, and hands. Though we are focusing in this chapter on windows, remember that parts of the body can give you insights but you must read the entire body to get the message just as you would need to read an entire sentence, not just a word, to understand a written message.

The shoulders and arms are the most visible parts of the body. They can normally be seen across a desk, above a counter top and on the other side of a table. While most of our eye contact during a conversation focuses on the triangle of the eyes, nose and mouth, we do spend a significant time studying the upper torso for information.

Symbolically the shoulders and the arms surround and extend out of the heart. Remember that body language is highly symbolic. Because these body parts come out from the heart, the arms and hands can be seen as expressions of what's in the heart. Arm and hand movements are the body's clearest emotional barometers. The shoulders, arms and hands are also considered the "doers" of the body, we use them to explore the world, and that is often where we look to see what someone is doing.

If a person wants to hide what he is doing or has done or hide his emotional state, he will close the window at the palms of the hands by hiding them. The most frequently asked question by participants in my public speaking classes is, "What can I do with my hands?" They long to have their hands hidden because they reveal the speaker's emotional state. In teaching interview and interrogation techniques, I have the law enforcement officers study the palms of the hands of the person they are questioning, as it is difficult to lie with the palms of your hands exposed. Liars tend to keep their hands hidden and still. They stick them in their pockets, clench them together or hold them behind their backs. Imagine that the person whom you suspect of lying has the truth in the palms of their hands and see if they show them to you.

The shoulders are the base for our head and the link to the emotional outlet of the hands and arms. If you examine the male and female silhouette, you'll see that males tend to have large, broad shoulders and women small, narrow shoulders. As women took on men's jobs during World War II, shoulder pads became popular in women's clothing. The female silhouette symbolically indicated its ability to carry the weight of work while men were away at war. When women began to take on more positions of management in the workforce in the 1980s, shoulder pads came back in style. Just like the powerful actresses of the forties--Joan Crawford, Barbara Stanwyck and Bette Davis--the powerful women on daytime television and nighttime soaps such as Dynasty wore shoulder pads as if to say, "I can be as strong and mighty as a man." Among other things shoulder pads make big-hipped women look smaller, so while their popularity may wax and wane, some women will always try to create that desirable hourglass shape that men find so attractive.

The phrase "you seem to be carrying the weight of the world on your shoulders" is said of round-shouldered people. People who seem to take on the burdens of life, or more responsibilities than they can possibly handle, will bend the shoulders over from the accumulated weight. The cartoonist captures this idea in drawings of figures coming out of a factory at the end of the day bent over from the work they've done.

When I was sixteen, I saw George C. Scott, who played the pompous General Patton on screen, play Willy Loman, the failure in the stage play Death of a Salesman. The first scene is supposed to show the quintessential defeated man coming home after being fired. His shoulders should have been slumped over with the weight of his failure, but the actor's pride and bearing made him lift his shoulders and hold his chin high as he came on stage completely changing our feeling about the character. This actor's body language was better suited to play a general than a failure.

People also will fold their shoulders in to protect their heart, closing their heart window. If that habit continues it affects the posture, so you can look at someone's habitual posture and see evidence of a "broken heart" or even an abusive relationship. Young girls may fold their shoulders forward because they are self-conscious of their breasts and wish to shield them from view. Some older people may stoop because of osteoporosis or lack of exercise. I have osteoporosis that causes a stoop-shouldered look, and in fact one of the reasons I am so drawn to body language is because I have learned that my large gestures and animation help to overcome the negative image of my stooped posture. Therapists say that one of the most accurate indicators that a client had an overbearing father or was or is in an abusive relationship is bowed or hunched shoulders.

As the saying goes, for the turtle to get anywhere it has to stick its neck out. The turtle hides by pulling its head into its shell. When we stand up straight with our shoulders back, we present a strong front. When we raise our shoulders up toward our ears in a shrug, we create an effect like the turtle's, lowering and protecting our head, retreating into our shell, or symbolically distancing ourselves from a situation we don't want or don't know how to handle. Often you will see the shoulder shrug combined with a head tilt and open palms, this combination of signaling sends the message, "I'm helpless."

Exercise

Think about your own body and how you hold your shoulders. Stand with your back against a wall in your normal relaxed posture. Do your shoulders press against the wall? Stand and then sit in front of a full-length mirror and examine your posture. What do you see? What silhouette are you showing to the world? What do you think it means? Do you think it has changed or can change? How do others respond to you? Shrug your shoulders. How do you look? Find some photos of yourself in different kinds of clothes, casual and dressy, how does that affect your posture?

Analyze

Think about someone you know whose shoulder posture seems to reflect one of the categories just presented. From what you know about the person, do the attitudes associated with the posture seem to be accurate for that person? In what way? How do you think his posture affects the way you respond to him?

LOWER TORSO AND FEET BODY WINDOWS

When you're reading body language, you read from the feet to the top of the head because the most honest portion of the body is from the waist down. When we feel safe, comfortable and relaxed, we tend to have our windows open. We typically only close down when we are tense or fearful. And since we are often socialized not to show our nervousness, those nervous, tense or fearful cues will often "leak out" through the feet.

Imagine you are talking to a man whose upper body is toward you but whose legs and feet turn toward the exit. He may be indicating that he wants to leave. When you notice this, you should consider the topic you are discussing and how the person feels about you. Then ask yourself if he is nervous and saying with his body, "I really want to be out of here." If he jiggles or taps a foot, especially toward an exit, he is symbolically running away. This also could be an indication of nervousness.

A "foot lock" in which one foot wraps around the leg usually at the lower calf is like having a "closed" sign hanging over the door. The person may be sitting with the rest of her body open, but the foot lock shows you her true fears. People who are relaxed will tend to take up more space with their legs. Especially when men stand with their feet far apart or sit with their legs apart, they are signaling that they are relaxed and confident.

The bottoms of each of the feet also have a window. A reporter from India was interviewing me at my house when she noticed my little shoe case near the door. "Do you take off your shoes when you enter your house?"

"Yes," I replied. "I love going barefoot, and it keeps dirt from tracking into the house."

She began to tell me about the custom in some parts of India of leaving your shoes by the door and putting on slippers to walk in the house. She said that the streets of cities like Baghdad are very dirty and the houses are holy places and you want to leave the filth of the street outside of the home.

I talked about the symbolism of the window at the bottom of the foot, that in American culture men often cross their legs, which shows the bottom of the foot to the person or people they are with. The symbolism says, "I am so powerful and strong, I could step on you if I wanted to." I asked about the taboo in Indian culture of showing the bottom of the foot. I had told my audiences for years that this foot posture was seen in Indian culture as extremely rude and insulting, but I had never known why. She told me that because the streets are so filthy, showing the bottom of your foot is like saying, "You are like the filth on my feet, I have no respect for you." What a great insight. This posture is considered rude in many other countries and by those of the Muslim faith. Such a simple posture, yet imbued with so much power.

Our body windows — upper and lower — show our degree of comfort about a situation or person.

I teach a college continuing ed class called "The Meeting of the Minds, and as the title suggests we get into some heated discussions concerning taboo topics like religion, sex and politics. We meet at a different coffeehouse each week and for the past nine years I have noticed the more potent debates start with everyone seated with their legs uncrossed, chairs tight to the table and their bodies bent over and leaning toward the other people at the table. I watch closely as a controversial topic is introduced. Then I will often see one person push back from the table, lean back and cross his legs or turn his feet away from the speaker. Immediately, I can identify the dissident thinker in that group.

Chapter 9

Talking Hands: Gestures

WHEN I WAS 13, I PLAYED HELEN KELLER IN THE PLAY, THE MIRACLE Worker. I was playing a character who could not see or hear and expressed her heart through gestures. As Helen, I flung my arms and hands up in glee; I swung them around to hit anyone who tried to hold me down. I grabbed for food off plates, clung to my mother so tightly the actress playing her complained, threw things with the wildness of an animal, and in the most pivotal scene, used my hands to feel the water in the pump, touch it to my mouth and spell out the word w-a-t-e-r into the hand of my teacher.

Abandoning myself to my emotions, free to fling out my feelings, I felt amazingly alive and filled with passion. The gestures poured out of me fast, like the water from the pump. My arms would feel like another living being that I somehow had learned to set free. Then I would walk backstage at the end of the play each night and know I had to stop moving. I had to leash my arms down to my sides so I would look normal and tame.   I have been teased all my life about my expressive and constant gesturing. When I was younger, my friends teased that I wouldn't be able to talk if I sat on my hands. Actually, it was very funny watching me attempt to stifle my hand motions. I would try to talk while sitting on my hands, but I bounced up and down a lot and moved my feet.

Why do I gesture so much? There are many reasons people gesture a lot — personality type, cultural upbringing, and more. I think one of the reasons for my expressive gestures is my early upbringing. When I was six months old, we moved to Wiesbaden, Germany. While my family worked, went to school and traveled Europe, I stayed with my wonderful nanny, who spoke only German. I learned to speak German before I learned English, so the only way my sisters and parents could understand me was through my expressive gestures. They called dinnertime with me "the puppet show," because I was so determined to express myself that my hands would dance to my German baby gibberish.

Analyze

1. Are you a gesturer or do you tend to keep your hands still. Mark on the continuum below what you think your degree of gesturing is during normal face-to-face interaction.

   --------X -------------X-------------------X------------------X ----------------X
   No Gestures Few Gestures Moderate Gesturer High Gesturer Extremely High
2. Growing up did your family gesture a lot?
3. How do you think your gesture pattern affects your communication and relationships?

WE ALL GESTURE ALL THE TIME

You don't have to have grown up in a foreign country to use gestures to make yourself understood. We all gesture, all the time, some more noticeably than others and some louder than others do. Our ancestors communicated through gestures for millions of years before we had words. It's no wonder we have an "evolutionary hold-over" to gesture.

In this chapter you will learn how gesturing can benefit you and how to read other people's gestures accurately.

Gesturing with your hands helps you

1. Let others know what you are feeling
2. Show people aspects of your personality
3. Communicate quickly and clearly
4. Increase your thinking ability
5. Add richness and creativity to your ideas
6. Communicate your conviction and confidence

Reading others' gestures can reveal all these things and tell us when someone isn't getting what we are saying.

THAT "WHOA" FEELING

Using your hands and other bodily gestures is a communication system all its own that works separately from, and in conjunction with, what you are saying. You actively express your emotions through your arms and hands. Your arms and hands project outward from your heart, and so illustrate how your heart feels about people and things. The gestures you use as you tell someone you care about them, the way you describe important concepts or a new work project, or how you use your hands when playing with a child, all communicate your emotions toward the people you are with and the ideas you are expressing. Your arms and hands may go out to hug a friend, cross over to close off someone, or playfully strike out at a teasing friend. Your hands tell the story of your heart.

Have you ever known someone who did the "hand jive" and talked with his hands? Actually, we all do. We bang on the steering wheel of the car when we wait in traffic. We drum our fingers on the desk when we're on hold on the phone. We jiggle our foot when we are eager to get out of a meeting. The physical movements we exhibit seem to match our psychological desire. We bang on the steering wheel because we feel like hitting, we drum our fingers in a desire to change the meeting to a faster pace, and we move our foot up and down to symbolically run away from a situation.

Because your arms come out from your heart, they show how open and receptive you are to everyone you meet and interact with, so when you hide them behind your back or glue them to your sides, you show you are not willing to embrace the person or the situation. Keeping your arms up and out shows you can be hugged. Personality tests say that the more outgoing you are as a person, the more you tend to use your arms and the more you gesture broadly. The quieter and more introverted you are, the less you move your arms away from your body. How do you gesture and what does it say about you?

Making it perfectly clear

Gestures serve all sorts of communicative functions. They link and support the words we say. Gestures can add meaning to something we say, give feedback that says we are listening, illustrate a point, provide additional information and can do it all quickly.

We use more gestures when we're excited or trying to communicate a difficult message. We reach into the world with our hands, expressing and caressing the air. Research shows that as we speak, our hands often enact the grammatical structure of what we are saying, showing particular movement with certain phrases or ideas. We might gesture with the right hand for one paragraph, the left hand for the next paragraph, and the next with both. We might search for our next words about our trip, twirling our finger forward like a wheel and then say, "…we drove on from there to Orlando." We might not even be aware of what we are doing but we do it skillfully. There are more than 100,000 possible hand signals using different combinations of postures, arm, and wrist or finger movements. No wonder we keep on doing that crazy hand jive!

As a professional speaker, I use an enormous number of gestures. Research says lecturers make twice as many hand gestures as people who are talking one-on-one. I attend the National Speakers Association convention each year, which usually attracts about 2,000 speakers. I'm always ready to jump out of the way from all the gestures people are making in the halls! Their gestures make them better "teachers." As a former university instructor, I think about the power of teachers' gestures. All of a teacher's body language affects their students in some way. In fact, according to research by Grant & Hennings in 1981, "82% of teacher messages are nonverbal and only 18% come from the words they say in class."

The Thinker

Gesturing actually helps you access information in your brain and helps you form your messages. One night after a week on the road, my body and mind were especially tired. As I began an after-dinner speech, I noticed I was having trouble thinking and wasn't as animated as usual. This was not good news as the audience had just finished a large steak and baked potato dinner preceded and followed by an open bar. They needed every bit of moxie I could muster to keep them from falling asleep in their apple pie. I increased my animation and gestures, and suddenly had no trouble speaking the words. They came out smoothly and effortlessly when only a moment before I was struggling. The apple pie and my speech were a success. I always recommend that you try to move around and gesture — even a little movement will help you verbalize (even if you're sitting on your hands).

Do people at work talk a lot on the phone? Watch their gestures. The next time you hear a heated conversation coming from the next cubicle, peek in and see which hand is gesturing. Using the right hand stimulates the speech centers in the left hemisphere of the brain so we can explain things logically and rationally. Using the left hand stimulates the emotional right hemisphere, so we can communicate our frustration. This may be dangerous as the only accessible verbal language in the right hemisphere is cuss words!

George Carlin has a classic comedy routine about a guy looking for his lost car keys. The guy keeps repeating the same hand in pocket gestures over and over while trying to find his keys. You've done that. You're walking around the house trying to remember where you put your car keys. You repeat your gestures and your movements, putting your hands in the pockets where you had them at one time, walking over to the kitchen counter and tapping the place where they should be but aren't, play-acting coming in the house the evening before and hugging your sweetie. You use your movement and gestures to help you remember. (By the way, the keys are behind the dog food, where they dropped when Fido greeted you.)

Gesturing may even help you remember things and let your brain rest. A study led by Dr. Susan Goldin-Meadow, the Irving B. Harris Professor in Psychology at the University of Chicago, shows that our gesturing helps us remember information.

In the study, 26 children and 32 adults whom the researchers observed using gestures went through a five- step exercise. First, they solved age-appropriate math problems. Then they had to memorize a list of items. In the third exercise, they were asked to explain how they had solved the math problems. That was a tricky part of the research. For the research subjects, having to explain increased the amount of work their brain had to do in addition to remembering the items. After that, they were tested on their recall of the memorized items. Finally, they were asked to give the explanation again, this time keeping their hands still on a tabletop, and were tested again.

The research found that on average, people who were allowed to gesture recalled 20% more items than people who were not. In a discussion of this research, another author, Dr Howard Nussbaum said, "These findings suggest that gesture reduces the cognitive load of explanation, freeing capacity that can be used on a memory task at the same time." Translation: gesturing frees up our brain.

Research shows bilingual people tend to use more gestures when they're speaking in their non-dominant language. So let's take this idea one-step further. If you're having a hard time expressing a point or finding the right words to say as you speak one-on-one, use gestures and let your arms and hands write out your message.

Exercise

1. Sit on your hands and face towards a friend. Now tell them how to get from your house to work, or describe where you played as a kid, or tell about your last trip. Did your hands want to help you? Was it difficult to talk?
2. With your hands free, say the following:
    - He came this close to my car.
    - Turn right at the next corner; go three lights then make a sharp left at the light.
    - The product line grew and grew and grew, and when it reached the very top, the bottom fell out and we got zero orders.
    - The fish I caught was this big — well actually this big.

THE CONFIDENCE FACTOR

I was sent photos of the Mayor of Washington, D.C. to read for the D.C. newspaper. In one photo, he has just given a speech. He is standing by himself on stage facing the audience. Two flags are behind him. His upper body is showing with his torso below the lower waist hidden behind a podium — more of his body being exposed than normal when standing behind a podium. His hands and arms are spread out above the waist with the palms open and his hands cupped upwards. He has a big smile on his face.

What does this mean?

This is what I call the "Jesus-on-the-cross arm posture." Reaching arms with palms showing are often asking for hugs, or sometimes to receive applause or in response to applause. The fact that he can hold this expansive gesture, exposing so much of his body in a large public setting, shows confidence. The smile on his face, the extension of the arms, and the upward cupping of the hands let us know he is enjoying himself and the kudos he is receiving. In fact, the upward cupping of the palms shows he wants to "hold" more applause. If the palms were facing flat towards the audience he would be signaling a humble request for the applause to stop. This is the body language of a confident man.

What would you want to see if you watched a tape of a speech you just gave at the quarterly meeting? Would it be seeing yourself gripping the lectern, fiddling with your shirt collar, clenching your hands together, clutching a magic marker or wiping your brow? I don't think so. You would want to see gestures that show you are confident and have conviction. You would want to see yourself opening and showing your palms as you say your opening statement. You might even lift your open arms up slightly to show your confidence. Finally, you would want to see solid intentional movements, like putting your fist into your hand, which forcefully shows you mean what you say, as well as smooth flowing hand motions that show an effortless transition to the next point.

When your listener is confused

A person's gestures can signal that someone needs more explanation. Another study by Susan Goldin-Meadow shows that teachers may pick up gesturing cues from their students that tell them the student is ready to learn. How would you know if someone you're talking to needs more explanation or is ready to learn? Look for a mismatch between his or her gesture and the words they say. If someone says the company will show a loss in the fourth quarter, but his hands gesture upwards, he is confused. This may sound really weird, but if your work requires that you train others and you run into gestures that don't seem right, you will discover magic teaching moments. If you're a salesperson, and your prospect is repeating a point you've made but the gestures seem out of synch, you know you need to clarify or risk losing the sale.

UNIVERSAL HAND AND BODY MESSAGES

While the gestures we use to communicate ideas and stories may be different for each individual, there are other, universal gestures to convey unconscious meanings, attitudes or emotions. Let me reiterate that, with a few exceptions, you shouldn't read any posture, motion, or gesture in isolation, but instead read the entire body language sentence.

Hands behind your back

In the UK, they call this The Prince Charles. When you hold your arms behind your back with your hands clasped, you're sending a gesture message. In certain jobs, such as police officer or Prince, this posture sends a message of power. But in others, the gesture makes you look untrustworthy. If we can't see what your hands are doing, we're suspicious. We think, "What he is doing back there?" So don't be fooled into thinking that keeping your hands behind your back makes you look cool. It you want people to trust you, keep your hands in view.

In another photo of the D.C. mayor, his arms were behind his back. In fact, his arms were so tightly held behind his back that his lower arms were hidden to the elbow. The shoulders were also pulled tightly back. These gestures were combined with other cues: of a lack of weight on his front foot and his mouth closed tightly, his chin jutting out and his eyes looking up and away.

These cues indicated his desire to back out of an unpleasant situation. As his arms were held back tightly and so much was hidden, it was obvious he was hiding strong emotions and not just impatience. Standing with shoulders pulled back is a retreating posture that says, "I want to be out of here."

Steepling Gesture
The word "steepling" comes from the word "steeple." In this gesture, the person is holding her hands together and linking fingers together so the knuckles point upward. Or, in another way, placing hands together and locking thumbs while the fingers point upward like a church steeple. In general, it means the steeple is thinking and processing information. There are several variations of this gesture.

The High Steeple
In the high steeple, elbows touch the table while the forearms are raised, causing the steeple fingers to point upwards. Both Churchill and Gorbachev used this steeple.

When I train salespeople in the pharmaceutical industry, I tell them that if they see a doctor go into a high steeple while they're presenting a new research study, ask the physician for his or her opinion. The high steeple is often used by those delivering an 'expert' opinion, such doctors, lawyers, academics or by people who have an "expert" or perhaps conflicting opinion on the topic. If you do not ask a question, the person with the high steeple will maintain his or her old opinion.

Low Steeple or the Cannon
This is a defensive steeple characterized by elbows touching the arms of the chair while the forearms and steeple point forward. The person using the low steeple has a strong differing opinion and wants to shoot "a cannon" at you. I actually coach executives, especially women who need to gain power, to use this position when they're under an unreasonable attack. I tell salespeople in my sales presentation class to be very careful not to use this gesture when responding to a question or comment from a prospect or an audience member, as it sends the message you would like to shoot them for talking!

Hidden Steeple

The hidden steeple is like the low steeple except that the hands are deliberately hidden below a table or desk. This one may be hard to spot, but if you see it, don't hesitate take action. It signals the person is confident in his or her ideas. It's a gesture I recommend if you are shy, lack confidence and just need to do an acceptable version of holding your own hand to feel better. I recommend to my clients that they put their hands in a steeple when they begin to feel a loss of control or power. The very act of holding the steeple can give you more control.

Praying Steeple

The name of this one should make the example pretty obvious. The praying steeple features hands clasped and upwardly pointed fingers, interwoven for prayer.

Crown Steeple

You see the crown steeple when the steeple fingers are unfolded or the interlaced hands are held high around the back of, or on top of, the head like a crown. The crown is one of my favorite gestures and one of the only gestures I do read in isolation. This gesture has meaning outside the context of the rest of someone's body language sentence.

I noted this gesture when I was giving my very first seminar on body language and began to discuss how gender and male power differences lead to sexual harassment problems. I looked around the room. I noticed that every male had his hands in some sort of crown steeple. As the name suggests, the crown steeple is also a power gesture. With the steeple, height comes into play. The higher someone holds the steeple crown, the more power that person feels or desires. Over the past 20 years, as women have come into equal positions in the workforce, men have steepled less.

THE CAPE AND CROWN GESTURE

You have all seen this one. You're out with a friend after the weekend. You ask, "How did your date with Jennifer go Friday night?" Before saying a word, your friend clasps his hands behind his head, extends his elbow on either side of the head and says, "Better than I ever dreamed. I'm seeing her again tonight." A steeple raised and locked behind the head, with the head tilted up and elbows extended, sends several power cues. The head is above the centerline, showing superiority. The V of the elbows extend outward, like a cape, take up lots of space making the person's head appear larger and elbow points are arrow like weapons pointing outward in attack. The hands locked behind the head indicate the person is locked in his or her viewpoint. The chest is exposed, puffed out and vulnerable, indicating a strong sense of personal power. The person comes off as smug and arrogant.

Just as we use gestures and touch to communicate to others, we also use certain gestures to comfort, control or communicate with ourselves. These gestures involve self-touch and serve as unconscious self-regulating mechanisms.

THE CAPE CROWN AND STEP ON

A female plant manager in my interpersonal skills workshop gave a look of shocked surprise when I talked about this gesture cluster. "Patti, now I know why I was sent to your program." I do this all the time whenever the supervisors come into my office or when I visit them. They get in the cape and crown and put their feet up on the desk and I follow suit. I thought I was just showing I was 'one of the guys' when I did that. Now I know it's a power gesture." Not only is it a power gesture, in her case it was a vying for power competition. The guys were showing a lack of respect by putting their feet on the desk pointing toward their manager symbolically saying, "We could step on you if we wanted to. Or you're dirt on our shoes." There was an additional problem with a female plant manager doing the gesture cluster. It's only acceptable in men. Women should never put their feet up. So she was also sending a male cue. We talked about how she could handle the lack of respect she was being given, and we practiced some other power cues such as taking up space and keeping her body windows open to replace this cluster.

MOUTH GUARD

This one I mentioned earlier. Covering our mouths is quite symbolic when we don't want someone to know we're upset, lying or if we're suppressing a negative thought. We put our hands over our mouths so the truth won't come out. Years ago, when I trained law enforcement officers in interview and interrogation techniques, we discussed the importance of watching the mouth when interviewing two suspects at the same time. Not only do people cover their mouths when they are lying, they will also cover their mouths when they are listening to someone they believe is lying. But it's not always about deception. In graduate school, I had a friend who would cover his mouth to speak if there were more than a few people in the room. I knew he was self-conscious because of the additional signals he exhibited, the shrug in his shoulders and his downward look. Always look for additional submissive gestures given with the mouth guard that may signal nervousness, shyness or a lack of self-esteem.

NOSE, EYE AND EAR RUBBING

Years ago, I was watching the Rosie O'Donnell show on TV. The guest was one of the actors on Ally McBeal. The tabloids at the time were hot with the rumor that Ally star, Calista Flockhart, was being treated for bulimia. Rosie asked Calista's co-star if this was a problem. He said no as he rubbed his nose. The topic came up again when Rosie touched some candy on her desk. The co-star said, "There is not problem." And the co-star rubbed his nose again. Finally, another guest came on. The question came up again and the co-star again said it was not a problem as he rubbed his nose.

These cues signify disbelief or disagreement: "Boy, that doesn't smell right to me, that doesn't look right to me, that doesn't sound right to me." Calista's co- star words were saying, "There is no problem," but because he was lying, his words didn't smell right to him so he rubbed his nose. Years ago, I mentioned these gestures in a large management workshop and noticed a participant rubbing his nose. Without calling attention to him, I added that research findings say that though you may scratch your nose because it itches, your nose may itch in the first place because the situation doesn't smell right to you. A week later, that doubtful participant called me and said, "Patti, I didn't believe those gestures meant anything until today. When I was giving an employee evaluation and it became negative, he started rubbing his ear. I ignored it and went on to the next point and his hand came down. I went back to the negative point and his hand went right back to the ear. I knew then he didn't want to listen to me on that point. He didn't like what he was hearing. I stopped and asked for his response and got some valuable in-formation. And his hand came down."

The neck is another area that lends itself to these types of gestures. I was conducting a team-building workshop for a food manufacturing company. One of the attendees, Bob, started complaining about a manager berating him about his last project. He went on and on about how out of line his boss was to give him such a hard time. One of his teammates, Ron said, "I know what you mean," and another teammate, Carl agreed, scratching his neck below his ear. Hmm, spotting the neck-scratch, a signal that said, "I doubt you or don't agree with you," I asked Carl whether he really thought the boss was out of line. "Not at all," he said. "Everyone who had to work with him on that project knows that Bob really messed up, but I have to work for him so I'm not going to say anything." Carl didn't say anything with his words, but his body language spoke volumes. But Bob wasn't listening.

FINGERS OR OBJECTS IN THE MOUTH

This cue links back to childhood, when we sucked a bottle, pacifier, thumb or our mother's breast. Self-touch gestures, like hands or objects in the mouth communicate a desire to find sustenance and comfort. So nibbling on a pencil or chewing on an eraser comforts us. If you see someone displaying this gesture, reassure him. If you are a salesperson, and your prospect starts to nibble on a pencil, discuss warranties and product quality, tell him this is a safe purchase to reassure him.

When Farrah Fawcett was interviewed on the David Letterman show, he asked her why she had chosen, in her fifties, to do a nude body painting video. She immediately put her finger in her mouth and comforted herself before answering. Chewing on a Styrofoam cup may reflect subliminal anxiety while violent chewing or crunching on ice may be a sublimated desire to take a bite out of someone. Biting or crunching on ice can also communicate high levels of anxiety. One night I had a writing deadline and should have been working on this book. Instead, I was watching TV. Halfway through the program, I noticed I was chewing my lip with anxiety. I turned off the TV, returned to my writing, and my lip was saved.

CHEEK OR CHIN GESTURES

Gestures around the part of the face usually correlate with thinking — stroking the chin, propping the chin in the hand, putting a finger on the cheek.

If you see these signals, ask yourself what you said or did just before these positive or negative motions:

- The head rests with its weight on the hand: boredom.
- Closed hand resting on cheek without the hand being used as support: evaluation.
- Chin stroking: the listener is making a decision.
- Putting a finger to the cheek: thinking.

A situation I found myself in recently not only shows the power of these types of gestures, but what can happen if we don't notice these gestures have changed.

At times I will go in and watch one of my clients speak before I begin coaching him or her. This gives me a chance to see how their presentations affect the audience and how the client responds to the audience. On one particular occasion, I was watching my client present to a group of 18 executives and technical professionals from a prospect company. He didn't have the client sold yet and this was the last presentation before they would sign off. As he spoke, the audience fixed their gaze on him. As they continued to listen, nearly all of them rested their closed hand with the index finger pointing upwards on the side of their faces. I was pleased because this gesture indicated they were very interested in the proposal.

Halfway through the presentation, the sales presenter mentioned an additional expense to the proposal because of increased prices in fuel. Immediately, one of the big muckety-mucks shifted. Now his thumb was supporting his chin and he crossed his right leg over the left. This body language shift mirrored a change of heart. The supporting thumb suggested critical evaluation and the crossed legs a defensive attitude. My client kept on speaking, not noticing the shift in a key decision maker. Then the shifter blurted out that the new expense should have been in the original proposal and an argument ensued. If the speaker had known ahead of time to look for disagreement gestures and had known how to respond to them, he more than likely could have prevented the argument. He could easily have said, "I see that this new cost is disagreeable to some of you," or "Let me explain it in more detail and tell you how we can make up your increased cost by speeding up the production time for you."

THUMB DISPLAYS

My friend Charlene, who reads palms, says that the thumb represents strength of character and the ego. Nonverbal interpretations say the same thing. "Thumbs up" says cool and good. We display them when we think we're cool or we want to be cool. Unless we're watching a cowboy in a John Wayne movie, we may interpret the thumbs up display as arrogance. If we see them protrude from someone's back pockets, the dominant feelings are being hidden, especially if the person rocks forward to give him self a little extra height.

RUBBING MOTIONS

These are more complicated. Rubbing may be a means of self-assurance, so we may gently rub a gold chain around our neck just before an interview, symbolically making it shine. A man may rub the end of his tie as he approaches his date's door, possibly indicating heightened sexual interest. In the old movie Cabaret, the characters sing a song about money. Throughout the song, they rub their thumb against their fingers as if they are expecting money. As we are about to be served a luscious dinner of lobster or a big dessert, we may rub our hands together in expectation.

Holding Motions

When we were little and we were anxious or scared, our moms or dads held on to us, and the holding motion assured us that everything would be okay. When we went to bed as children, we may have held onto a teddy bear or a blankie to reassure us that everything was all right. As adults, when we are anxious or afraid, we repeat these motions to reassure ourselves that everything is going to be all right. We may hold our hands together, grip our arms in a self-hug, or hold a pen or marker as we speak.

A colleague of mine does career coaching for laid off employees. She shared with me that they're often so traumatized by their terminations that they can't make eye contact. They look down a lot and during tough questioning, they fidget or wring their hands, which shows their anxiety.

Preening Motions

To prepare yourself for an interaction, you might fluff your hair, rub out the wrinkles on your pants, or adjust your tie. These self-touch motions offer comfort to us and may subconsciously remind us of when our mothers used to do these things for us before an important event such as the first day of school.

Remember, no body language is good or bad. It's okay to do all these things. Johnny Carson, loved by millions and earning millions, grabbed his tie during his monologue and played with a pencil during tough interviews. David Letterman holds his Top Ten blue cards. I recommend that my nervous speech students use a prop they can hold for a moment, especially during the particularly tense beginning moments of their speeches, or keep a nickel in one pocket that they can return to and hold onto to anchor themselves throughout their speech. Some things we've held continue to hold a special meaning for us. We often keep the stuffed animal, the blanket or the pillow we had as a child.

Palm, hand and arm gestures

An open palm facing upwards or your palm facing away from the body indicates honesty and openness and can make you look friendlier ("I am open to your ideas" or "I am not so sure"). Making gestures with your palm down can make you look dominant and possibly aggressive, especially if you don't bend your wrist ("I order you" or "I am sure")

Now, I am not a big sports fan, but I am fascinated by athletes' body language. Have you ever noticed that every time football players trip an opponent or foul them in any way they quickly raise their hands, with their open palms facing the referee, symbolically saying, "I didn't touch him"?

Our body language shows that underneath our skins we still carry the mannerisms of our ancestors, the apes and other animals. Just like a male bird fluffs his feathers to make him self appear larger and impress a female or to intimidate another male who intrudes in his territory, guys will puff up their chests and put their hands on their hips.

Pointing

One of the first things most of us learned about body language is that it's not polite to point. Why? Pointing is a potent gesture of power, a symbolic weapon. When you make a fist and thrust your finger out, you're symbolically shooting someone. It's threatening.

When Former President Bill Clinton turned to the nation, pointing his finger and said, "I never had sex with that woman," he was lying. This is often the case, especially during testimony in front of congressional committees. So, does pointing a finger mean you are lying? Absolutely not. The average Joe would never do that. In fact, when I teach law enforcement, I say pointing can be a sign that someone's telling the truth because they are passionately defending themselves. I do see pointing used by powerful men like Clinton, who are used to getting their way and who have lied successfully in the past. They use it when they are cornered to defend themselves by counterattack. Notice this when you're watching speeches and news clips. This is such an interesting phenomenon that I did an entire segment on it for FOX news. I read clips of Clinton, Nixon, sports figures, and a congressman who was accused of racketeering. The timing of the point was often the give away. When someone is telling the truth they feel their emotion, then they show the emotion, then they speak. The power pointers often say their false message first then point. A classic historical example is Nixon's pointing in his "I am not a crook" speech.

Everyday speakers use a different version of pointing to show conviction of thought. They will point with passion just a beat before they say the powerful statement.

International gestures

There are a few words that are so simple to you may think gesturing will easily communicate them. However, beware of this idea because gestures are also an "in country" language.

Let's say you are up at the front of the room and you notice that the lights are dim and you need them turned "up." Simple, right? Just point at the light switch at the back of the room, take your thumb and swing it up and down a few times. If you're speaking in Australia, pointing your thumb is rude, and if you move your thumb up and down, you have just told your audience, "I don't respect you. Up yours." In Nigeria, this is also considered rude. If you're speaking in Japan, your upraised thumb means "one" and in Germany, you look like you're signaling "five." In England, talking with your hands in your pocket is impolite.

If you're working in a foreign country, find out if there are gesture signals that you might use in your work that could be misconstrued.

Tips

Here are a few more tips regarding body language gestures:

- If you're a women and want to catch a man, use this provocative self touch cue. Touch your neck at the collarbone, just about where a necklace would sit. The neck is a vulnerable location and touching that weak spot lets men know that you can be approached and touched. Touching or caressing a necklace is also provocative.

- We use gestures as well as words to let someone know we have a question. To indicate that they are asking a question, a person may give a little jerk of the hand or thumb, or a jerk of the head. They may also signal it's your turn to talk by raising an eyebrow, and or jerking the head sideways or jutting the chin forward as if to say, "Tag — you're it."

- To tell if someone is truly excited, notice his or her hands. Sometimes they will use hands to create an exclamation mark in the air, or they will do chopping movements up and down or sideways. If these motions are overly forceful they should be read as symbolic weapons and you should watch out!

Explore

Imagine walking into a room and seeing a long lost friend you haven't seen in years. What does your body do as you approach your friend?

Imagine someone you don't like coming into your cubicle to talk to you. What happens to your hands and arms?

Imagine sitting next to someone with whom you've had an argument. What does your body do? Where do your arms go?

Put your hands in a high steeple. How does it feel?

Analyze

Did you have a comforting object when you were a child? Do you have something in your home or office now that you like to pick up and hold that offers you comfort? Have you ever found yourself holding on to a magic marker during a speech?

Chapter 10

Reach Out and Touch Someone: The Power of Touch

I THINK THAT TOUCHING IS THE MOST IMPORTANT NONVERBAL skill, and so I think this is the most important chapter in this book.

I am somewhat biased in my thinking. I was lucky enough to receive an abundance of touch as a baby and child. I am the youngest of three girls. My parents tried for nine years to have a third child until I finally came along and they were overjoyed. My mother says I was so loved and held so much that my feet didn't touch ground for three years! And with two older sisters, I really grew up with three moms. Add to that a German housekeeper who thought no child should be left crying, I was cuddled, hugged, played with, and loved on a lot. It made me the touchy-feely member of the family.

It continued as I was growing up. I was tucked in to bed until I was 10. I hugged my parents all the time. When my dad came home from work, I still ran to the door to hug him. I kissed him goodnight until he passed away when I was in college. Now, when I visit my mom or my sisters we always hug and kiss on the cheek when greeting and again with our goodnights. If that sounds like a lot of touch, it really isn't. It's just a few touches a day, just a few seconds in 24 hours of living.

In this chapter, you will see the benefits of touch. The research on how touch affects your development as a baby and child, how it affects your health and social skills, how touch affects business interactions and a myriad of other things is stunning. You will also learn some simple steps to add more healthy touch to your daily life. You'll learn ways to use touch to affect you and everyone you interact with in a positive way.

I teach in my workshops that the average 18 year old has heard the word no 80,000 times. Wouldn't it be great if the research said the average 18 year old has been hugged 80,000 times? It takes the same amount of time to say, "No Son, you need to stop doing that. I mean it" as it does to go hug your child before they do something bad to get your attention.

Touch is perhaps the best way to communicate. During a study where subjects were only able to communicate using their hands, people were able to communicate five separate emotions: detachment, mothering, fear, anger and playfulness, using only their hands.

It starts early

My friend Justin and his son Chris have an incredible father and son relationship. The first few times I saw them together, I noticed how loving their relationship was. They would wrestle with each other like bear cubs, laugh and tickle each other. Jeff would rub the top of Justin's head, wrap his elbow gently around his neck to pull him in close, and hug him close to say good night.

Seeing this loving affection made me cry the first few times I spent time with them. I cried because Justin adopted Chris from the foster care system when Chris was ten, and I know how lucky both of them are to have found each other. Justin went through training and coaching on how to care for Chris's special needs before he adopted him. He learned that children from homes where there was abuse and neglect need to experience touch at the most basic levels in their new families, because they missed it growing up.

I talked recently to Justin and he shared, "Chris was physically abused and neglected as a child, but I was told that of the two, neglect is actually the worse form of abuse. It causes more problems." Chris's birth mother was an alcoholic and drug addict and left him locked in the house for weeks at a time when she went on binges. Justin said, "He missed all that loving touch."

"My mom is a social worker and with her help and what I learned from my training and research I knew I had to start the touch at square one. I needed to give him all the touch a baby would have gotten normally. So we all gave him baby touch. I pinched his cheek and told him he was cute. I played goochy goo, I cupped the top of his head and kissed it. Of course, my mom and dad did all that with me when I was a kid. I knew what healthy touch was. The thing is, he ate it up"

"It's funny," Justin continued. "It seemed impossible to me that kids who were beaten actually have fewer problems than kids who were neglected, but now it makes sense. At least when they were hit they got attention. Horrible, isn't it?"

Chris is fourteen now. Touch is still important. Remember, he has only gotten the touch a four year old would have received. The research says Justin and the rest of the family need to continue to give Chris touch that children his age have normally "outgrown." Justin says, "If he is angry at friends or at something that happened at school, I just hold him in a hug and he immediately calms down. His whole body relaxes."

Justin also says he becomes a baby when he is sick. "If he wakes up in the middle of the night and he wants a drink of water, he calls for me to bring it." He can do it himself, but when I bring it I put my hand on the back of his head and put the cup up to his mouth just like he is a small child. The moment he lies back down he is totally calm and serene. He knows what we are doing. He knows that that not all fourteen year olds would like that, but he enjoys it, because he never had it."

"What's really amazing is that nonintentional touch affects him so positively. When I am giving him a haircut, he balks and makes a fuss to avoid getting his hair cut, but when I start touching his head and turn it, he calms down. He gets this happy face and acts like he could sit there for hours. I think he gets a sense he is loved."

Justin philosophizes, "I think Chris would have been okay in a house with a parent who wasn't as comfortable with healthy touch, but I don't think he would have come as far as fast as he has."

And there are some great signs that Chris has learned how to touch in a healthy way. Justin said, "When I got him I was told to watch for signs that he might abuse animals. Kids who are neglected and abused can do that."

"I saw how great he was with my friend's dogs and I got him a dog when he was 13. He strokes her head and belly. He loves to give her bath and take care of her. The dog Dixie raises her paw, taps to say, 'Pet me', and he does. Chris just eats it up. He responds to the dog's message of 'I am a helpless being, take care of me.'"

Chris is at an age where most kids will pull away. But Chris doesn't. He still needs it and it's a good thing for him. And though our touch phobic culture says don't give touch to older children, for Chris, that touch is critical. Justin says, "In a public setting he doesn't shy away from my arm being around his shoulder. He still pulls my arm to come see something he wants. He still holds my hand walking across the parking lot." Justin and Chris are rebirthing a life. They are filling it up with everything Chris missed.

Justin's words of advice: "It is never too late to grab that grown kid of yours and kiss them good night. It's not too late to hug your fifteen-year-old teenager." I agree. It's not too late to build that love. They will receive it. No matter what your age you want to be accepted. And when somebody touches you in a loving way, it shows they care about you on a deep primal level.

Research done across centuries and around the world has proven what most of us realize the first moment someone puts an arm around us, reaches across the table to hold our hand, or envelopes us in a hug: there is great power in a single touch.

Researchers have proved that touch makes us better communicators, better friends and better people. Touch is vital to our physical and emotional development and to our overall sense of health and well-being. Touch is at the cornerstone of a healthy relationship with others, and with the self. Touch is, quite simply, remarkable.

The benefits of touch

Touch is positive. When one person touches another gently, briefly and on a non-sensitive part of the body, the interaction (even without words) is always positive. Only when people perceive a touch as a status or power play or when it is too prolonged can it create anxiety or anger.

According to biobehavioral scientists at UCLA School of Medicine, touch is critical to a baby's brain development. Developmental neuroscience research finds that the infant brain is designed to be molded by the environment it encounters. In other words, babies are born with a certain set of genetics, but they must be activated by early experience and interaction. In the critical first months of life, vents are imprinted in the nervous system.

"Hugs and kisses during these critical periods make those neurons grow and connect properly with other neurons," says Dr. Arthur Janov, in his book, Biology of Love. "You can kiss that brain into maturity."

The first portion of our brain to evolve on top of its reptilian heritage is the limbic system, the seat of emotion. It is this portion of the brain that permits mothers and their babies to bond. Mothers and babies are hard-wired for the experience of togetherness. Breastfeeding, co-sleeping, and baby carrying create bonding through touch.

Most mothers instinctively place their babies to their left breast, keeping their hearts close to the babies. The heart produces the hormone ANF that dramatically affects every major system of the body. Evidence indicates that the mother's developed heart stimulates the newborn heart, activating a dialogue between the infant's brain-mind and heart and the mother's heart.

According to Tiffany Field, PhD, director of the Touch Research Institute at the University of Miami, "Cuddling stimulates pressure receptors in your baby's skin that create a host of effects, including reducing levels of the stress hormone cortical, lowering heart rate and blood pressure, and improving digestion." It works the same in adults.

The same goes for the benefits of massage. Fields says, "Babies gain more weight, sleep better and relate better to parents. Their brain waves indicate more alertness, and they learn faster. Kids with Attention Deficit Hyperactivity Disorder or autism also become more attentive. [Massage therapy] alleviates depression, too. It decreases stress hormones and increases serotonin, the body's own antidepressant. It also improves sleep." Fields also points out that massage helps the immune system, and helps decrease autoimmune problems such as asthma. With massage, immune cell counts improve in people with HIV. A breast cancer study showed massage increased natural cancer killer cells.

Amazing.

What happens when we're not touched?

Touch not only feeds basic physiological needs it also provides physiological needs. It gives reassurance and comfort and aids in the development of self-identity and self-esteem.

Did you know in the 19th century, more than half of all first-year infants died from a disease called Marasmus, also known as infantile atrophy or debility? They later discovered that the infants had one thing in common: a lack of touch. Babies who were not touched on a regular basis would literally starve themselves to death.

Touch deprivation impairs development. For example, Romanian nursery children have been found to have a higher than average incidence of stunted growth. When given massage therapy, they showed improvement. A control group got attention but no touch and did not show the same improvement.

If you're looking for answers to increasing violence in the workplace, consider this:

"Touch deprived infants and toddlers become aggressive children," Field says. "As a culture, we are not gentle and physically demonstrative enough with our children." Out of eighteen industrialized nations, the United States tops the list in adolescent male homicides. France — one of the huggy-kissiest countries around — is at the bottom. Studies conducted in McDonald's restaurants and playgrounds in both countries show American moms to be less physically affectionate with their kids than French mamas.

In a 1990 study of 49 nonindustrialized cultures, groups showing physical affection toward children had little or no adult violence; in groups that were less affectionate to kids, adults were significantly more violent. Some suggest that the absence of physical affection affects the wiring in the brain that later creates the aggression.

Do you think the same doesn't go for adults? Do you think that perhaps we could use a little more gentle touch in our workplaces and our relationships? James W. Prescott, Ph.D., says, "The easiest and quickest way to induce depression and alienation in an infant or child is not to touch it, hold it, or carry it on your body."

All this is true and yet we have a created a no-touch culture. Our fear of sex, sex offenders, and sexual harassment means nobody wants to touch. My sister, a middle school math teacher for over 20 years (after which she achieved sainthood and retired), said that she was not allowed to touch her students. I was appalled. I did some research and found that in her state, there was a statewide "no-touch" policy and that these "no-touch" policies are now followed by caregivers, teachers, and other child workers around the country. Can you imagine being with children eight hours a day, five days a week and not being able to give a loving, supportive touch? To me it seems monstrous! And these policies are growing in popularity. I was recently watching the 1980's movie, Three Men and a Baby. There is scene where two bachelors, having found their roommate's baby left on their doorstep have to change the baby's diaper. Asked to wipe the naked baby with cotton wipes, one bachelor asks the other, "Should we be doing this?" It says a lot about our no-touch culture that we fear the simple act of changing a baby because of sexual taboos.

If you're interested in exploring further, read the book, Hands Off: The disappearance of touch in the care of our children, by Richard T. Johnson. It will make you want to hug your children and write your senator.

Touch reduces stress

Research links the quality of the touch in your adult life to the competence you have in your relationships and the stress in your adult life.

Study after study has found that social ties reduce our risk of disease by lowering blood pressure, heart rate, and cholesterol. "Loneliness is the leading cause of death in this country ... I don't know anything in medicine — not drugs, not surgery, not diet, not lifestyle, not genetics — that has a greater across-the-board effect," say Dr. Dean Ornish, heart specialist and author of *Love and Survival: 8 Pathways to Intimacy and Health*. To add emphasis, Ornish says that loneliness and isolation increase the likelihood of disease and premature death by 200 to 500 percent. We need closeness and intimacy in our lives. Sometimes, I think that our need to indulge in hours in front of the TV, an evening of cocktails, an afternoon of shopping, or a meal of too many calories is our attempt to fill up the emptiness caused by a lack of touch.

TOUCH BENEFITS IN BUSINESS

- In a classic library study, when a librarian touched students (both male and female) on the arm for a fraction of a second while the student checked out a book, the students rated the librarian, the library and the overall experience more positively
- In a study in restaurants, waitresses (surprise!) got significantly higher tips when they gave a fleeting touch.
- Students ranked tutors who touched lightly on the forearm as more positive and supportive.
- Giving a brief touch has been shown to make you more attractive and persuasive.
- Touch: a cultural comparison
- Rates of touch per hour for adult couples in coffee shops, frequency of contact: zero in London, 2 in Gainesville, Florida, 110 in Paris, 180 in San Juan, Puerto Rico.
- Cross culture similarities — Most cultural expressions of emotion seem to indicate that touch and positive attitudes go together, while touch and negative attitudes do not. For example, winning football and basketball players pat the posteriors of their teammates, while losers don't. In research on swimmers, winning swimmers gave and received a significantly greater number of touches than did last-place finishers.
- United States norms of touch — When asked who got the most strokes (physical touch or signals to show I know you're there), 44% of those surveyed said their pets got the most strokes, 18% said their children got the most strokes, and 18% said family members got equal strokes.

Touch do's

There is a movie called Love Actually that ends with a montage of airport greetings. The montage is filled with joyous people hugging, kissing, and smiling the most incredible smiles. Just watching that montage is uplifting.

As a weekly flyer for over 20 years, I love watching the hugs and loving touches given to travelers in airports. Before security measures disallowed, loved ones would meet each other just as they got off the plane and the traveler who had looked tired and depressed just moments before would transform as they kissed their sweeties, lifted their children into the air, placed toddlers on their shoulders. The trip to baggage claim was happier for all of us as we caught the joy of these loved ones ourselves.

In the Atlanta airport where I arrive as a weary traveler, we have a long walk and train ride before we see our loved ones. I ride on the train with sad and exhausted travelers, all wearing what I call "Friday Faces," the tired look of someone who has worked and traveled all week and is just barely hanging on until the weekend. But when we reach the top of the escalator, there is a sea of loved ones, holding, "I love you" signs and carrying roses, ready to touch and hold us and transform our Friday Faces to faces full of love.

By the way, there are studies on this too. In one study done at airports, 60% of people engaged in touching when greeting or saying goodbye to another person.

Types of touch

To encourage touch, you must know what is safe and non-threatening.

Men differentiate what your intention is by the way you touch more than where you touch them. Women differentiate what your intention is more by where you touch them than by the type of touch. Patting is associated with play, but you have to be careful where and whom you pat. Guys can pat other guys on the back and shoulders and women can pat other women in those same locations. But because women notice where you touch them, guys cannot pat a woman at the office high on the arm near the women's chest, unless they want to risk it being misinterpreted.

Stroking, as in moving the hand across an arm, though associated with warmth and love, is also associated with sexual desire. So though it would seem natural for a nurturing woman to comfort someone with this kind of touch, it is not appropriate for her to touch a man that way in the office. He might notice that type of touch and think, "She wants me!"

Touch to-do's

"How about a hug?" Ask for hugs and give them freely. There are many forms of affection — cuddling, a pat on the shoulder, etc. Find out what kind of affectionate touch the people in your life want and give it to them. At Florida State, though I did not have a doctorate, I was called Dr. Hugs by my students. My nonverbal communication class had more than100 students, so everywhere I went I got a hug. I loved it.

"Thank you." Touch can be a reward. A gentle touch on the forearm or hand at work or a hug or kiss at home can let people know you appreciate them. Think of all the little things people do for you and reward them with a touch. I was "the napkin girl" when I was very small and after I went around the table folding and putting the napkin at each place setting, I got a hug. As I grew older and set the full table, I still got a verbal thank you, but the hug was absent. Continue touching to say thank you. Heidi Feldman, chief of the Division of General Academic Pediatrics at Children's Hospital in Pittsburgh says, "A child is much more likely to try to please a parent who acknowledges his contribution and thoughtful, helping behavior."

"Tell me more." I did research in grad school on touching to increase self-disclosure. Sure enough, when you touch someone even briefly in a non-threatening, non-sexual way, they will self disclose more. This was helpful for me to know and take action as a therapist, but just think how powerful it is to use in your personal relationships. We tend to skate on the surface of our relationships instead on becoming emotionally intimate. Create the intimacy of pillow talk without sex by giving healthy touch to encourage people to share more. There are places and times where "Tell me more" touch works very easily. While cooking or eating dinner with loved ones, you can purposefully touch as you hand each other food, plates and utensils, When riding in a car or golf cart, you are close enough to touch in a non-threatening manner, even if it is something as innocent as passing a drink or handkerchief. In sales or other meeting settings, you can touch when passing out handouts, brochures or samples.

"Let me comfort you." Sometimes we move away from loved ones who are highly emotional, crying or upset when moving in closer and touching can help them feel better.

There is an exception to this. Therapists are sometimes encouraged not to touch too soon so their patients can stay upset long enough to share all their pain. When my best friend Roy was dying, one of the worst things to deal with was the lack of comforting touch I could get from others. I moved to Atlanta away from my other friends and family and the one person who normally hugged me and gave me the most comfort was Roy. And he needed me to be strong for him. If you know someone who is going through grief and loss give them comforting touch. So often, we get caught up in taboos and avoid the natural inclination to touch. People will step back or arch away if they are uncomfortable with the prospect of your touch, so take the step to try it, knowing you can move out of it if you need to.

"You can do it." Use touch as a motivator. Touch as you give a work assignment, as you put your child on their first two-wheeler and as you send your sweetie off to his or her first marathon. Touch makes us feel empowered and is a great encourager. Increased self-esteem received through touch can help others follow through a challenging task. I spent a lot of my teenage years working on plays. I remember clearly how we would all hug each other before each play started and would give little back rubs to actors about to go on stage for a difficult part of their performance. The touch fed us and made us strong. Think of all the touch given in a sporting event. It's not surprising the encouraging touch given to athletes is similar across cultures. We know that a pat on the back moves a person forward.

"Please." Use touch to ask for help as well. It won't surprise you to know that pairing touch with a request makes it much more likely the person will do what you ask. Just a brief touch on the forearm, lasting less than a fortieth of a second, can increase your persuasive powers.

"I love you." It should be very clear to you now we need physical contact to feel acceptance and belonging. We all want to be loved.

Touch and power

We tend to consider the person who initiates touch to have higher status. Bosses, doctors and professors commonly initiate touch. The person who initiates touch generally controls the interaction. However, that doesn't mean that powerless people don't touch. Women initiate touch more than men and women touch women more than men touch men. And same sex dads touch more than opposite sex dads.

In his book *The Right Touch: Understanding and Using the Language of Physical Contact,* Stanley E. Jones describes a study of a public health organization: "The group studied was a detoxification clinic, a place where alcoholism is treated. This was an ideal setting in which to study status, sex roles, and touching.... [The] findings showed two clear trends. First, women on the average initiated more touches to men than vice versa. Second, touching tended to flow upwards, not downwards, in the hierarchy."

'Non-reciprocal touching' refers to instances where one person touches another, initiating the contact and not getting touched back. Nancy Henley, in the classic Body Politics said men use non-reciprocal touching behavior on women, implying it was a gender difference. I think it is just a power difference condoned by our culture. Men are most likely not aware that they can do this or that it can come across to women as a physical sign of control and dominance. Though 'touching' might sound like an easily identifiable form of harassment it can be more subtle. Notice what goes on in your day-to-day life. Do you see men or women 'cuddling', poking in the ribs, lifting up, grabbing, touching and 'tickling' their opposite sex friends and colleagues regularly?

I have mentioned I read the body language in photos, and clients will sometimes ask me to read the family photos on their desk. In those family portraits, the fathers often have their hands on the shoulders of their wives and children. This is top down touch, a power touch that shows the men's power. If the hand is cupped and the rest of the body language is warm and caring, this touch can show fatherly protection. If the hand is gripping and the rest of the body language is overbearing, it can mean that this is man is The King and controller of his castle.

I read the photo of an Atlanta coach for the local newspaper. The coach was touching the face of his star player. His hands actually cupped the face of the player gently as he smiled at the player. It was a tender and loving touch, but you can bet the player did not reciprocate the touch!

Notice how coaches or bosses, those in more powerful positions might touch, pat or rub the heads or shoulders of less powerful others. In these instances, the boss may push the person down, showing their power over that person. There may be many instances in which these touches are reciprocal and/or experienced positively. However, it is the unwritten rule that more-powerful people can touch us in a way that we may not touch them.

Evaluate

How often do you touch others during every day interactions?

Exercise

Beginning this week, consciously watch how and when you touch. Alternate days when you touch more and touch less, for instance, on Monday touch people more often than usual, on Tuesday touch them less than usual. See if this makes any difference in how you perceive how your day went.

Body language knowledge self test

Check the appropriate response:

1. You're at a wedding reception and Lisa, one of the bridesmaids, makes eye contact with your single friend Mark. As Mark approaches and tries to make eye contact with her, Lisa looks down and away and then turns to talk to someone next to her.
    ___Lisa wants to meet Mark
    ___Lisa doesn't want to meet Mark
2. Frank is in the middle of a long day of sexual harassment training. As the speaker begins talking about inappropriate behavior, he twists sideways in his seat and begins blinking a lot.

___Frank is bored out of his mind

___Frank knows he may need to examine some of his behaviors at work more closely

3. You are interviewing a candidate for a management position in your department. As she comes in the room, she shifts her purse to her other hand to shake hands, then makes three attempts to find a place she wants to set it. Then she puts down her briefcase and adjusts it so she can search through it for a pen and paper. Finally she looks up at you and smiles.

    ___You say to yourself, "She's out of the running."

    ___You say to yourself "Let's see how the rest of interview goes."

4. You go into your bank to apply for a home equity line of credit. The bank manager smiles and says brightly he will be happy to help you. As he pulls up your credit history, he starts rubbing his eye. As he looks down at the paperwork, he hands you a pen and asks you to fill it out. His voice going down in volume.

    ___You know he will do all he can to help you

    ___You realize you're sunk

5. At the store there are several checkout lines available for you to push your cart. At one the cashier is cleaning the belt; she glances at you and then back down to her cleaning. At another the cashier is talking animatedly to one of her coworkers and at a third the cashier makes eye contact with you and then faces her upper body towards you.

    ___You chose the first

    ___You chose the second

    ___You chose the last

    ___Nobody smiles so you decide to walk a little further down

6. You are at Blockbuster Video with your six year old; you are holding two movies that you want to rent. As she looks at them, she first bounces up and down and smiles. Then she looks away and sighs audibly.

    ___You realize she was excited to see you had picked two movies but she didn't like your choices.

    ___You realize she is excited and impatient to check out

    ___You realize you do not have enough information to make a judgment

7. You walk into a meeting and notice that as you sit down your manager adjusts his paperwork stack that is facing you and adds a book to the top of it. He moves his stapler a little more towards you and then he sits back in his chair.

    ___You sit down to talk.

    ___You ask if there would be another time to talk.

    ___You know that this is not a good time to talk and excuse yourself and leave

8. You are arguing with your spouse about how much money you should take from savings for your vacation when your wife puts her hands on her hips and juts her chin out.
   __Look out. Your wife is really mad now
   __Your wife is afraid

9. You walk into your assistant's cubicle, and standing beside him, you point at the computer screen and tell him what he needs to change in the format.
   __You are being friendly and direct
   __You are being intrusive

10. Molly and Ron are sitting at home watching television when Molly says, "Let's go out to dinner this Friday with Elaine and John." Ron doesn't answer.
    ___He didn't hear her because he was focused on the last two minutes of the game on TV
    ___He doesn't want to go
    ___He is mad at Molly

Answers

1) Look past the first cue given. You need more information before acting. You may think by looking down Pat is shy and wants Mark to be the aggressor, but the withdrawing of eye contact, combined with the resounding message of turning to talk to someone else should signal Mark that she does not really want him to approach her. She may have just been initially friendly, but she did not back up her original cue.

2) The timing of cues, that is when they started and with what speed they occur, can help you with your accuracy. Frank's blinking and sudden posture shift alert him that he is uncomfortable with what the speaker is saying and that instead of turning off, he needs to tune in and see if he may have acted inappropriately at work. Franks knows he is not bored, because his cues are fast and came on suddenly as soon as the topic shifted.

3) Don't Base Impressions on Stereotypes. If you dismiss this candidate thinking she is overly spacey or nervous or weak, you may miss out. You may have just witnessed a gender difference: women on average in such a setting have 10 times the nonverbal movement cues than men to settle themselves into a chair and start a meeting. Ideally, you will give the benefit of the doubt and see if her movements seem strong and confident as the meeting progresses.

4). Again, don't go by just the first cue given. Noting what came before the shift in body language will help you read this bank manager accurately. Though he was initially friendly using a bright tone and giving you a smile, you realize that your credit history must be bad because just after he looked at it his behavior changed from enthusiastic to doubtful (rubbing eye) and disinterested. (voice suddenly losing volume and energy)

5) OK, this should have been an easy one. The first one may have been the most sanitary wiping down her counter, but by looking down she said she wasn't ready for you. The second cashier was friendly to her coworker but ignored you. And even though the third cashier didn't smile, you should have chosen her because by turning the upper body toward you, she showed she welcomed your approach.

6) Mixed signals tell you that you do not have enough information. When you present lots of information at once or a list of choices you may get mixed responses. Don't assume that she was excited because you had picked two movies but she didn't like your choices or that she was impatient to check out. She may have given two responses - one for each movie. Hold the movies up separately and you may see that she wants to see Ella Enchanted and doesn't want to see the Olsen Twins movie.

7) Notice the details of people's cues. And check for the motivation. Though someone may adjust things on their desks to make you feel welcomed, those adjustments usually are about making more room and taking down barriers. This guy was making his castle wall higher and adding a cannon as enforcement. You shouldn't take this personally. It is likely that something is going on with him. For example, he may be busy at the moment and not want an interruption so you need to see if this a good time to talk or if he is actually busy. As a further check, if you think it is a time constraint, notice whether he does this every time you come in to talk and whether he does it with anyone else.

8) People naturally try to appear bigger to get power and actually appear smaller when they feel powerless. Hands on hips and jutting chin are ways to make someone appear bigger and more threatening. You wouldn't naturally exhibit those cues if you were frightened.

9) Having power does not give you the right to invade space. Our cubicles are our kingdoms. And you just came in without knocking or asking if it was a good time to talk. You are also standing above your employee, emphasizing your power difference. You had to lean over his shoulder to touch his computer screen, which puts you into a personal space we usually reserve for more intimate relationships. And finally you touch his computer screen, which he may see as contaminating his belongings (especially if you leave a fingerprint smudge!). This is not friendliness. This is intrusive behavior!

10) Consider the context of the situations before jumping to conclusions. This should be a gimme. What was Molly thinking — it's the last two minutes of the game!!!! Ron is focused on the game. Rude, perhaps, but Molly could have brought up the question at half time.

Chapter 11

Matching and Mirroring

I WORKED MY LAST YEARS OF COLLEGE DOING TELEPHONE SURVEYS for the governor's office. Yes, I was the person interrupting your dinner to ask you questions about how many refrigerators you had in your home, whether you owned a boat and what you thought of the waste water sewage treatment in your area — you know, all those fun, stimulating topics. And I had to keep you on the phone for 45 minutes. I had to read straight from a script, with no add-ins or improvising except for my greeting and goodbye. Our supervisor listened in to check for cheating.

I loved this job. I am not joking. I really enjoyed it. However, most of the surveyors didn't. They would sigh, curse and bang down the phones, stressed out that someone had hung up on them. Most surveyors lasted for one or two survey topics — one month and they were out of there. I couldn't figure out why everyone else seemed to get all the bad "callees." Mine were so nice.

Because we were doing scientific research, we had to complete all our calls. My boss started giving me the "hang-ups." That meant I would call people who had hung up on other surveyors and get the person to complete the call. I was good at this, so I got a raise. Soon my salary tripled and I was calling people who had hung up on surveyors four and five times. I would get them to complete the surveys.

So now you're wondering how I did this (or am I just bragging). Well so did I. Then I took my first nonverbal communication class and I learned about something called matching and mirroring. It 's a natural phenomenon that causes you to match the body movement, voice tone, tempo and breathing of people you like. It also includes liking and feeling comfortable with the people who are matching you. That was what I was doing naturally on my phone calls without even knowing I was doing it! If the person picking up had a light, happy voice, I said hello in a light, happy voice. If they answered with a quick, loud hello, I matched with a quick, loud hello. If they breathed fast in the first few moments of the call, I did the same. If they paused a lot and breathed deeply and so did I. These people felt comfortable and safe with me. They felt, at the subconscious level, that we were from the same tribe, so they stayed on the phone, telling me about their boats and wastewater sewage.

You experience this phenomenon at work. Someone comes into the office in a seriously bad mood. They walk down the corridor of cubicles and without even making eye contact, their bad mood spreads like the flu. This pull towards the same energy is called isopraxism. It's one of the reasons we get so excited when attending football games at a stadium. We see the aggressive body language on the field and it charges us up. We sit close and tight next to others and it charges them up. Soon we're all jumping out of our seats, yelling and screaming with the crowd. When I was at Florida State, we called our Saturday night football games, "Saturday night fever" — the games were that exciting. We did indeed "catch the fever." I always thought "the wave" at the games was one of the clearest examples of that pull towards the same energy. Holding your stadium cup and your hot dog, you would see the wave coming around and say to yourself, "That is so lame, there is no way I am doing that. As it drew closer, you were still saying "absolutely no waaaaaaayyyy" as you were pulled into the wave, spilling your beverage in the process.

So this is interesting information. You don't have to have someone screw up her face in anger and yell at you to get you going. She can just walk by and contaminate you. As I say again and again, you have the power to impact everyone you come into contact with, negatively or positively. You can do that with Matching Magic

MIRROR MIRROR

Real communication — verbal and nonverbal — means being able to see the world both through your eyes and someone else's. Communication is about creating understanding. Rapport is the fastest and most effective way to create understanding with another person. Neural linguistic programming (NLP) offers a way for us to create rapport consciously using nonverbal communication to match or mirror another's body language.

Rapport creates a feeling of trust and safety between you and the other person. Rapport means the other person feels heard and understood. When you are in rapport with another person, you have the opportunity to enter their world and see things from their perspective, feel the way they do, get a better understanding of where they are coming from, and as a result, enhance the whole relationship.

Matching creates friendships

My best friend Roy and I had incredible rapport with one another. We would dress in a similar way — same dark blue jeans, same leather jacket. Both of us even had red shoes, mine pumps and his oxfords. We would sit in a similar way next to each other on the couch. When we got on the phone, we talked in a similar tone and rhythm. When we were sitting across the table from each other eating, we would both pick up and put down our knives at the same time. Our sameness made us feel comfortable around one another. Being with each other was like being home. My roommate in graduate school wrote her Master's thesis novel based loosely on our lives as roommates. Her professors said that my eerie matching with Roy did not make sense. So in the novel she made us twins!

Analyze

Do you have or have you ever had someone in your life that moved in sync with you and made you feel comfortable and at ease?

Not matching creates enemies

I once had a nemesis at work. I felt I was nothing like her. We didn't dress the same, she carried herself with southern charm, was soft-voiced and slow moving. I was a cockeyed kid, fast and furious and full of fire. She annoyed me. Being around her for any length of time made me feel miserable. Her southern slowness and sugary smiles appeared false to me and I didn't trust her. And I bet I annoyed the heck out of her. What was the underlying problem? We didn't match, so it was very difficult for us to have rapport and difficult for us to trust each other.

Analyze

Have you ever noticed someone who did not match you — someone who had different postures and gestures and voice patterns than yours? Did you ever think that there was something wrong with them, or that if they would just be a little more like you things would be a lot easier?

Matching creates trust and self-disclosure

Matching and mirroring are taught has part of FBI and law enforcement training. By matching the suspect and/or witness you gain trust, and they are more likely to share information. You can begin to "feel" what the other person is feeling.

There is another interesting aspect of matching physiology. Do you remember when I explained the connection of body and brain? The concept is whenever we hold and move our bodies in certain ways, we create specific chemicals in our brain. Therefore, we feel and think the way we hold our bodies. Now, imagine that you can successfully match someone's physiology. You create the same chemicals and the same thoughts. And those chemicals shunt into your bloodstream in less than a fraction of a second. You can begin to feel what they are feeling.

When I was a counselor for substance abusers, I was trained to match and mirror my clients' body language. It successfully let me understand their feelings and gain rapport with them, but it was difficult for me to complete a day of counseling without feeling drained. I hadn't learned how to come back to myself, to my own body language.

Match can change emotion and persuade

You have an upset customer in front of you. Your remaining calm isn't working. They are red-faced and yelling, and their hands are gesturing wildly. The worst thing you can do here is yell back. Instead, match the intensity of their nonverbal behavior and bring your volume up slightly as you bring your hands up to slowly gesture and say with intensity, "I understand that you're very upset." As you continue to do this for a moment or two they should feel a match, which in turn will make them feel heard and understood. While you're talking with them, slow down your rate of speech and bring down your volume level. Do this slowly and begin to make small changes. People yell loudly and keep yelling because they don't feel heard. Ideally, they will not need to yell any more because you matched them. They feel heard and understood. As you slowly move to a calmer set of body language and vocal cues, they will come with you. Voila, Magic Matching!

Matching can create romance

You can match and mirror on three nonverbal levels: body language, voice and breathing. An unusual phenomenon in this process is that while you're consciously matching and mirroring someone, he will not be consciously aware of what you're doing. Simply smiling when he smiles or nodding when he nods creates a mirror image of his posture. Matching the physiology will operate very powerfully on the other person's subconscious. She will think things like, "I feel comfortable," "I feel good," "This person and I seem to have a lot in common" or "I like this person." If you use this method with integrity, others will feel comfortable with you. And it doesn't take very long. You can match someone for a moment or two and create rapport. You do not have to match every move someone makes for three hours. You can create rapport in less than a minute.

Years ago, I was at a museum gathering with a tall friend named Carol. Across the lobby I saw a tall, dark, handsome stranger. We smiled at each other and he approached us, accompanied by his shorter male friend. I am 5'1" and was with a tall friend, so I knew I was going to get the shorter guy, even though I wanted the tall, dark-haired one. The shorter guy was very cute, but blonde. In all my years as a body language instructor, I couldn't ever remember consciously using matching and mirroring to catch a man, but now was the time. As the tall one leaned to the side, tilted his head, and put his hand on his hip, I mirrored each action, including the tone and pitch of his voice. I was smitten, and it came out naturally. The tall one asked me for my business card, much to the chagrin of his short friend, whom I found out much later had said he wanted to date me as the two approached us. My tall guy later said he agreed to let his short friend ask me out, but as he and I had spoken, he came to feel that we were such a good match he had to ask me out himself. That matching is pretty powerful stuff! In fact, I consider it so powerful, I haven't consciously used it to catch a man since.

In that illustration, I matched the tall guy's body movements and his paralanguage. You can also match someone's breathing. When we are completely relaxed, we breathe down deep in the belly, just like a little baby's breath. This breathing allows us to take very full breaths and completely fill up our lungs and exhale all the carbon dioxide. When we're neither completely relaxed nor tense, we breathe from our mid-chest, and when we're nervous or tense, we breathe faster and high in our chests, above our heart level. Obviously, matching someone's breath can really tune you in to him or her.

Ways you can match

So, let's discuss ways in which you can consciously match or mirror to create rapport. To do that let's first distinguish between matching and mirroring.

Mirroring is acting as if you are the mirror of the other person. If they move their right shoulder and lean to their left, you mirror and lean your left shoulder and move to the right. If they lift their right hand, you move your left.

Matching is moving the same part of the body they are moving in exactly the same way. They lean back; you lean back. This is what I did with the tall man in the story. Typically, in mirroring, you mirror at the same time as the other person moves. In matching, you wait until a bit of time has passed or wait until it is your turn to speak before you match.

Matching body language

Body language includes facial expressions, eye movement, gestures and postures. But start out with one behavior at a time with one person and slowly move up to match multiple body postures and movements as you become more comfortable.

MATCHING VOICE

I called my usually warm and wonderful friend Pat, but I knew even though she was talking to me, that she really didn't have time to talk because she didn't automatically match my voice as we began to talk. Sure enough, when I checked in with her, she confirmed that she didn't. We've all done that. You are on the phone with your friend or your sweetie and something does not seem right. Your friend is probably not doing what would come naturally — matching your voice tone, tempo and speaking rate. By the way, people who do not have time to talk will mismatch without even realizing they are doing it. We know subconsciously that being out of sync with someone it will feel more awkward and the phone call will tend to be brief, and that matching makes the other person feel more comfortable and the call will be more likely to last. Notice in your next few phone calls how the voices change when you or the other person is ready to end the call.

When I was in grad school, I taught in the speech department at Auburn University in Alabama. Very quickly, I began to naturally match and mirror the speech patterns of my students. I slowed down my rate of speech and lost my "g's". So I said huntin' and fishin' rather than hunting and fishing. It was the right and natural thing to do. It was a wonderfully warm and relaxing way to talk. My northern-sounding (make that Florida) speech was too fast and too clipped for me to be accepted. I would have been strange and different, and my students would have had a harder time warming up to me. I would have had a harder time persuading them to become better speakers. Now you might say, "But you were a speech teacher." Well, creating rapport and connection with others is not just the most important thing you can do one-on-one. It's also the most important thing you can do with an audience.

You may have noticed that when you visit relatives from another part of the country or from another country altogether, you tend to take on their accent or rate of speech. It's a way of showing that you care.

For voice, you can match tone (i.e. harsh, sarcastic, and assertive), speed (fast to slow), volume (from soft to very loud), rhythm (the beat and emphasis), accent and clarity or articulation (how crisp or slurred the c's and k's sound). Don't match so quickly that it sounds like you're making fun of them. You don't have to match for very long or match completely. Stay in a zone that's comfortable for you. For example, if someone is speaking much louder than you, you could just get somewhat louder. It doesn't have to be a perfect match.

Match sounds breathing and pacing

This is the trickiest thing to do well, but it creates the most magic. You actually match the person's breathing rate, including ways they breathe as they speak. When you do it well, you will almost immediately get a rush of the feeling that person is feeling. If you think matching breathing is odd, remember, you already do this all the time.

TIT-FOR-TAT MATCHING

I used to love to watch Johnny Carson's Tonight Show as a kid. He was a masterful interviewer. Then at 11 years old, I wanted to grow up and be the female Phil Donahue and get to interview all those interesting people (Oprah beat me to it!). Once I learned about matching and mirroring in college, I watched Johnny and Phil with a more critical eye, trying to discern what made them so successful and how they got people to feel comfortable and self-disclose. I discovered they both were masters at tit-for-tat matching.

In tit-for-tat matching, one person does one thing, such as shake their crossed foot up and down. In response, you do something else like drum your fingers at the same pace. Or they might pick up a coffee cup and play with it, so you pick up your sunglasses case and play with it. My favorite little Carson magic trick was something he did to get his guests to match him and pick up the pace. Whenever he noticed the interview was dragging he would take a pencil and tap it front end to back, up and down like a seesaw, to the pace at which he wanted his guest to speak. His guest would immediately pick up the pace. It was hysterical to watch. Once I knew to look for it, I saw it almost every night. Johnny and his number-two pencil conductor's baton really made for great TV. In tit-for-tat matching you have rapport but you do not create the same emotional feeling in your body as they have.

I mentioned that as a substance abuse counselor I matched and mirrored my clients so well I felt depressed and drained at the end of the day. It made me an empathetic counselor, but I had to change my career choice. I didn't know then that if you do purely tit-for-tat matching, you can make the person feel rapport but prevent yourself from getting pulled into anyone's negative feelings. Use tit-for-tat along with other matching or when you're with someone whose emotional state you don't want to assume.

MISMATCHING

When I was in high school, I would wear mismatched, crazy looking socks every day. I didn't want to get sucked into the preppy, everybody-looks-like-a-Stepford-teenager thing. It certainly made me stand out as different. You can mismatch your voice, breathing and body language when you do not want to get pulled into another person's thinking or emotional state. You can mismatch when you don't like someone and you want to make it perfectly clear. You may do this and not know it. When someone is really into the conversation and talking fast and gesturing with enthusiasm and you sit back in silence and keep your arms still and give no facial feedback or sounds. You can mismatch to shut down aggressive salesmen and pushy coworkers. If you have a tendency to want be nice you may be subconsciously match everyone, even people you do not like. To reduce the length of negative interactions, you may have to do what I do and focus consciously on mismatching. It can certainly help you get out of those tricky situations.

Stay real and all will go well

At this point, you may be thinking this is going to be uncomfortable, that you will get caught matching or the person you matched will feel manipulated. Remember, you do this naturally a thousand times a day. It will come across well if you come from a place of integrity and are matching to make the other person feel more comfortable. I did research in Grad school on matching and was amazed that out of the hundreds of students that were matched in the lab only two subjects knew that they were matched. And these were people sitting in a lab room on the other side of mirrored wall.

They were looking for unusual behavior. When you begin to use matching consciously, start slowly. Try matching some little action today and then one more tomorrow and so on. Start with people you know and then move on to strangers standing in the checkout line or sitting next you on the train, plane or automobile. Increase your conscious control over your matching. You will be amazed at the results.

Exercise

Sit facing a partner. Partner A is the leader and you are Partner B, the matcher. Have Partner A sit on the edge of the chair, with his body tense, tight and folded. Now, slowly and carefully begin to match what Partner A is doing with his body. Once you have matched and begin to feel in sync with Partner A, slowly and carefully move out of the match. Let Partner A know at the outset once matching has occurred, so he can do whatever seems natural. Now switch roles and repeat the process.

What did you notice? Did Partner A, who was matched, move along with Partner B as he pulled out of the match? Did you feel the tug to match your partner as he pulled out of the match?

Explore

1. The next time you are sitting in a meeting with strangers, or perhaps when on an airplane or in a waiting room, slowly begin to match the person sitting next to you. Start at the feet and move up through the torso, then match the placement of the arms and hands. Finally, see if you can breathe the way he or she is breathing. You may be surprised to see how quickly the person you are matching responds and starts a conversation with you.
2. Here's a rather daring exploration, but very telling. Come home from work one day and let your body language be the opposite of the body language of your sweetie, roommate or family member. So if she is pumped up, be slow. If she is mellow, be hyper. If she is happy, be brittle. It should only take a moment before something happens because she is probably used to you getting in sync with her right away. It's a powerful exercise. Sometimes the person will match you; sometimes the person will get agitated. We are so influenced by the people with whom we keep company.
3. The next time you are around a close friend or perhaps a group of friends, notice if they are matching and mirroring.

Analyze

Get out your old photographs and see if friends and family members are matching and mirroring each other's postures.

Chapter 12

Smile and the World Smiles With You

MY MOTHER SMILES AT EVERYONE. SHE WAS BORN AND RAISED IN Windber, Pennsylvania. When she took her nickel up the hill to the little grocery store, Mr. Conjackos gave her a sincere smile. When she went back the next week, he was there, smiling as always. When she went down the hill to get a square slice of pizza, the counter guy, Sam gave her a big smile. Over the years, her father saw the same people every day at work. He always gave them a big smile. It was easy. And the salesmen at his soft drink company who called on the same customers for years always had a smile for them. We know that people smile more at people with whom they are familiar than at strangers. Being raised in a small town my mother got a lot more smiles than many people do today. And we know that our smiles bring positive reactions that usually reinforce them. So my mother learned that her smiles would be rewarded. And to this day my mother lights up any room she enters with her smile.

You've experienced it, too. You come into the office with a real big smile on your face and suddenly people respond to you with a smile and seem to treat you better. It's a well-researched social phenomenon. Research shows just looking at photos of happy-faced people makes a person's brain waves go to a happier mode. And similar research shows that seeing a smile can give you more pleasure than money, sex or eating chocolate (Ladies, I know it's hard to believe that anything is better than chocolate!). A smile is nature's peace symbol. It is our most frequently used facial expression. It is polite, disarming and not threatening.

Smiling may be the most powerful nonverbal communication cue we have.

When do you begin smiling?

Though babies aren't born smiling, it doesn't take long for them to start doing so. About three weeks after birth, and probably after a good burping, babies give a fleeting smile in response to touch, sound and visual cues like the funny faces and sounds you tend to make. They start recognizing faces and start smiling to get you to smile and treat them well at about 8 to 12 weeks. Just about when you are tired of getting up at three in morning and changing their diapers, the baby wins you back with a smile. A child's smile gives the same level of stimulation as eating 2,000 chocolate bars or receiving $15,000 in cash.

Do we "learn" to smile? Some of you might say that babies learn to smile because they see others smile when they do. Or, you might say that they see others smile when they are enjoying themselves, so the baby puts that technique into its personality bowl. And you might be right, to an extent. What we have found is this: though ways of smiling and some aspects of social smiling are taught, even babies who are totally blind smile in response to voice or tickling.

I know an interpersonal communications consultant who says he can figure out how well people work together in a company within one hour of walking through the door. What's the first thing he looks for? He says he counts the number of smiles he sees within the first 15 minutes. People who are glad to be somewhere or especially glad to see each other will smile. Even when you are attending an important meeting where you know in advance you will hear bad news, people will still smile during those moments before the meeting begins.

Somehow, that ability to "socially smile" so that others will want to treat us well can be hammered out of us at work. Someone comes in the office and asks us how the day is going and we grimace downward. We ask somebody to make us 200 copies, but because we're in such an overwhelmed state, we don't take the time to smile during the request. And then we wonder why the person doesn't hop to it. If your boss smiles at you while saying nothing, you can still feel appreciated. If he or she doesn't smile while saying, "you did a good job," it just doesn't feel right. As we said earlier, it's not your words; it's the nonverbal communication.

In the last year of my best friend Roy's life, he was in and out of the hospital. My emotions, as you would expect, were in turmoil. I would wake up in the morning and cry, get in the shower and cry, get in my car and cry.

Here is the weird thing. I smiled and laughed when I was with Roy. I would walk through the solemn halls of the hospital ward, everyone hushed, tense-faced and subdued and feel absolutely depressed. But being with Roy could be wonderful; we were so grateful to have one more day together. We would joke around about foods we could slip into his IV feeding pack like menu items to order at the drive through at Wendy's. "Patti, do you think you could sneak a 'Frostie' into the IV pack?" The staff, of course, thought all our smiling was insane. After all Roy was dying. We thought it was natural; we had always made each other smile.

It's a natural reaction. All of us have been caught in that awkward position when attending a funeral or visiting someone who is gravely ill at a hospital. We walk in the door, see somebody we know or haven't seen in awhile and wonder how to greet them. Do we suppress the smile that comes from seeing an old friend or family member? After all, society or cultural rules say it wouldn't be appropriate to smile during such an occasion, but we want to anyway. I personally plan on having funny hats, big red noses, and plenty of smile-inducing chocolates prepaid for at my funeral. I want everyone eating chocolates and smiling.

Here are some interesting and important points to note about smiling.

How do you smile or what defines a smile?

You can use over 80 different facial muscles to smile. We typically see smiling as a spreading and upturning of the lips. It changes the face significantly enough that it can be detected and recognized after three seconds from 300 feet — the length of a football field. Sounds incredible, doesn't it?

Why did our ancestors need to smile?

Though they did not attend a lot of cocktail parties where they needed to smile and make small talk, our caveman ancestors did run into other cavemen they did not know. So they smiled as they approached a stranger, basically saying, "I am harmless. Don't pick up your spear and kill me." In fact, smiling is the oldest form of expression used to show a desire to cooperate. So even when the smile was a football field away, the cave man noticing that smiling person approaching his cave, knew the smile meant the person was safe and he shouldn't be afraid.

Does a smile mean that someone is happy?

No. There are over 50 different types of smiles. We smile not only when we are happy but also when we're feeling a multitude of other emotions as well. This may make it difficult to tell what someone really means when he or she smiles. According to Paul Ekman, the father of facial expression research, there are more than a dozen different positive emotions expressed with various smiles. If you know what specific part of the face to look at, you can tell whether someone is really smiling from happiness or not.

To tell if someone is giving a sincere smile, look at the eyes, not the mouth. When looking for a real smile we usually look for a zygomatic smile. Such a smile uses the zygomatic major muscle that runs from the cheekbone down at an angle to the corner of the lips. In a zygomatic smile, the lips turn up significantly at the corners and the cheeks seem to lift up. This smile makes us look happy. When media outlets like US Weekly send me photographs of celebrity couples to analyze, I look first for that type of smile.

The lower part of the face, however, is easy for someone to manipulate. The person could be giving a fake smile. The upper part of the face is key. We often look for the little wrinkles at the middle outside corner of the eyes. Most people call them "crow's feet," but I call them "happy feet". The actor, Michael Douglas, inevitably has those wrinkles when he has his beautiful wife, Catherine Zeta-Jones on his arm. Still, this may fool us. We really don't know just by looking at crow's feet if someone is happy or whether he just wants to look happy.

Typically, when someone is happy, their brow lowers and their eyes seem smaller. So look specifically at the muscles that surround the eye socket. The muscles around the outer part of the eyes are hard to consciously control; only ten percent of the population can do it. A real smile, one that comes from joy, contracts the circle of muscles around the eyes. Keep looking at the brows overall and see if they lift from the person's normal resting position.

Movement is key

If you are with a person as they smile, look for the wave. No, not the football stadium arm wave. We're talking about the face wave. Real smiles seem to crest over the face like a wave, changing very rapidly from a small facial movement around the lips, lifting the sides of the face and the eyes and then the brows into a broad open expression. Put your hands flat over your face right now. Let your face relax. Now think of a cute puppy, your favorite sitcom star, or say money and smile. Did you feel your hands move up? Did you also notice saying the word money creates the wave? Kind of funny, isn't it?

Timing is important

Just like other facial expressions, the combination of the smile with the person's words and emotions will tell you if it is heartfelt. Typically, it goes in this order: a person will feel happy, smile and then say something happy — Feel-show-say. If you ask them if they are in a good mood and they say, "Sure," but hesitate and then smile, they are not feeling very smiley.

Listen to the voice

The timbre of the voice during a real smile is so distinctly different from that of a fake smile that the blind have no trouble distinguishing the difference. You can tell when someone is smiling when you talk to him or her on the phone. We can tell whether someone is giving a real smile just by listening to the voice. Research shows if you smile when you record a clear friendly message, there is a greater chance that your customers will leave a message in return. This is even true of your most reluctant customers.

You may have heard of customer service training that makes call center workers look into mirrors and smile when they are on a call. Many participants in these courses ask the instructor, "How the heck can the customer tell the service person is smiling on the phone?"

When we smile, the muscles around the voice box relax, making your voice sound warmer and friendlier. This smile comes through on the phone.

Does it pay to give real smiles?

Combined open-mouth cheek-raising smiles are more "emotional positive." They make us feel better than those smiles that feature only the open mouth or only the raised cheeks, or neither. There are long-term benefits from real smiles as well. Experts coded women's smiles in their yearbook photos. Women who gave real smiles were compared to those who didn't. Years later, those with real smiles overwhelmingly had happier lives.

Most smiles will pay off. Fake, forced smiles may not have the power of real smiles, but oddly enough, they're still better than full-force, negative facial expressions. Smiling in general makes us more persuasive.

See if these facts make you smile:

- People with less power smile more often than people with greater power, using this as a strategy to get what they want.
- Happy people smile more often during social interactions. Smiling, which to most of us indicates at least a minimum degree of good mood, has proven to lower heart rate and produce less stressful and rapid breathing.
- Research also shows that when we do smile, it produces the emotion most closely related to it, feeling happier.
- In marketing, a smiling face is more effective than a non-smiling face in eliciting both a positive attitude towards the smiling person and a positive attitude toward the firm using the smiling campaign. This positively influences the viewers' intention to use the firm and/or buy the product.
- Nonverbal behaviors such as nodding and smiling overcame status differences for lower-status people

People like real smiles and have harsh reactions to insincere or inappropriate smiles. In situations where happiness is inappropriate, happy smiling people are seen as more manipulative, suspicious and overconfident and are often judged as less likeable than those who act less happy.

Do men and women smile differently or for different reasons?

You know the answer to this one. Any man who has heard his wife say, "Everything is fine" as she presses her lips together tightly, with the corner of her lips raised slightly, knows that women fake smiles more than men do. And he knows he'd better watch out!

- Women not only fake smiles more than men do, they are more aware of smiling. They are more likely to stop smiling in private than men are.
- Men as a gender are uncomfortable around women who aren't smiling.
- Men are often concerned that their smiles will make them appear less powerful. This makes sense. Men with higher levels of testosterone smile less often. This is rather sad. If you smile less often, you tend to have fewer close relationships with others.
- Overall, women smile more than men do.
- Women maintain community by smiling while men maintain dominance when not smiling. This desire to maintain community may explain why women smile more in formal settings than men do by an overwhelming 77% to 35% margin. In casual settings, it's a little closer, 92% to 70% with women still smiling more.
- Another reason we might consider for this phenomenon is that women who smile are seen as more attractive. Even ninth-grade boys and girls picture the ideal women as smiling. Take a look at teen magazines and count the number of boys and girls who are smiling.
- Men learn they're supposed to give a serene smile in response to stressful situations. Women don't have to do that.
- Men who smiled more during video interaction were perceived as having more power; women were seen as having less.
- Research shows that women in business are more often told to smile than businessmen are.
- Shy women smile the most of all women. In that case, the smile is used as a defense rather than to open up. A shy smile or nervous smile derives from social pressure and hostility. Women might be more self-conscious than men; and pressure to be pleasant can make women smile to "cover

up" their nervousness. Not surprisingly, in primates, showing the teeth held together is almost always a sign of submission.

I do a survey in my all-female audiences. I ask them how many have been asked by men, "Why aren't you smiling?" or have just plain been admonished for not smiling by men. Every woman raises her hand. And just before they raise their hands, there is always a scary sound of frustration, to show this just plain gets their goat. This is usually followed by a very lively discussion and inevitably we talk about how often men tell us to smile!

Do Americans smile more or differently than people in other cultures do?

Americans smile more often and are more likely to simply part their lips and stretch the corners of their mouths to smile. We give a lot of fake smiles.

Though the British have a refrained, dignified smile, they are more likely than Americans to smile by pulling their lips back and upwards, exposing their lower teeth and doing the eye-changing, real smile. The French rarely smile at strangers and tend to think Americans who smile the entire time look ridiculous; but once they know you, they will smile just as positively as anyone. In some cultures, people will put their palm in front of their face to cover an embarrassing show of emotion given by a smile. In Korea, smiling can be seen as something shallow people do. In Indonesia, the resting position of the face is very often a smile.

Just as the Cheshire cat left its mysterious smile behind when it left, the smile has a lasting effect on us.

Why do we feel better when we smile?

There is a two-way street between pleasure centers in the brain and facial muscles. We feel good when we smile, but we can get the same result by putting our faces into the smile position. This position signals the brain that you feel good so it sends "feel good" chemicals into your bloodstream. Even when we are asked to smile, we still feel more favorably towards the people we are with. We also think funny things are funnier.

There is actual circuitry in the brain set up to respond positively to a smile. And then there is the facial feedback loop. We mimic the facial expressions of people we like and want to empathize with them to feel what they are feeling. So when they are smiling and we mimic it, we feel great.

Can we smile through our tears?

I was sitting in a park reading a book when I heard a child's painful scream. When I looked up, I saw a mother running frantically to help her 4-year-old child who had fallen and banged her head. As the child wailed, the mother did what mothers do, comforting and holding the child. Then the mother stopped and pointed to a crack in the concrete near where the child had fallen and said, "Look! When you fell, your head cracked the ground! Look what you did. The ground feels worse than you do!" This absurd notion brought an involuntary smile to the child's face, even as the tears continued to fall. The child apparently realized this and tried to fall back into crying mode. At that point, the mother said to a friend, who had also run over, "Look, Hannah cracked the ground! What a hard head she has." Hannah smiled again, tears still streaming down her face. No matter how hard she tried, it just didn't hurt as much as it had.

Research shows that faking laughter and smiles doesn't help pain tolerance. But the people who really smile, showing the true smiles around the eyes, did have higher pain tolerance. This means when they were truly happy and truly smiling they were able to produce an analgesic effect (something mothers seem to know instinctively). And the pain tolerance with a true smile has been shown to last 20 or 30 minutes. In some cases, it's doubled the subject's pain tolerance.

Why is this? There are several guesses. Some say it produces endorphins in the brain. Another says it increases serotonin and dopamine, which we have learned affect our emotions.

What do smiles say about your marriage?

Happily married couples shower each other with real smiles (described earlier) at the end of the workday and unhappily married couples do not. It's as simple as that.

Exercise

1. Next time you're at a gathering, whether business or social, alternate greeting people with and without real smiles. See if you get different reactions.
2. During the next week, observe the way you feel when with people you really like and when with others. Be more conscious of how you smile. Even if you're not looking in a mirror, you can tell how your face feels when you smile.

Chapter 13

The Eyes Have It

IMAGINE YOU ARE A SUPERVISOR. YOUR DEPARTMENT HAS GROWN and so you need to select an employee to take on more responsibility. You know the person you choose will need leadership abilities. You have narrowed your search down to four equally trained employees. In talking with them, they are all saying the right things, but you notice their eye contact is significantly different.

Employee A has an unblinking stare with small, contracted pupils.

Employee B is looking at you approximately half the time when they are speaking and about 75 percent of the time when you are speaking. He tends to focus on your eyes and the bridge of your nose.

Employee C looks at you normally most of the time. Her gaze tends to hover at your mouth and nose. When you talk about longer hours and supervising others, her blinking rate increases.

Employee D looks at you about half of the time with her gaze focusing on your eyes and nose. Occasionally her eyes narrow slightly when you're talking.

Whom would you have chosen? Read the rest of the chapter to find out how accurate your assessment is. I bet you did well. We subconsciously know and respond to these cues all the time.

Eye contact can determine others' responses to you

During a high stakes poker game on television featuring professional card players, one of the players is wearing sunglasses. Is it a showy prop? Or do the glasses give him an advantage? Research shows professional poker players win fewer games when their opponents wear dark glasses. The reason? They can't observe their opponent's eyes, which clue them in on his next move

Think of all the phrases we have regarding the eyes — "bedroom eyes," "shifty-eyed," "give 'em the evil eye," "twinkle in his eye," "teary-eyed," "sparkling eyes."

A friend told me about a coworker who came to him complaining about her employees. His coworker said, "I go in and hand them assignments and they either hand them in late or not at all. I am doing their work." My friend said the problem his coworker has is the way she asks.

"She walks in and starts talking, without making eye contact. Her voice is even. She faces towards the employee, which is great, but as she continues to talk, she still doesn't make eye contact. She looks at the document in her hands as she points stuff out to the employee. She looks at her shoes, she looks at the employee's chest, stomach, and even back towards the door but not at the eyes of the person. I always watch, because it looks weird." No wonder her employees don't follow through. The coworker doesn't make a connection. In fact, her eye contact was submissive, and so they weren't compelled to take her seriously.

Your gaze sends a message of power. It also gives you control of the conversation whether you are the speaker or the listener. To build rapport you need to gaze at them about 60 to 70 percent of the time, intermittently looking away. If you are not sure if you look enough, ask yourself if you're getting the attention and results from people that you want. Eye contact sends the message that you are serious. If you're still not sure, ask the people you interact with whether you give enough eye contact.

You need to make good eye contact with others. A lack of eye contact can make you look dishonest, disrespectful, evasive, rude, incompetent, lacking in confidence or lacking in conviction. In North American culture, we expect people to look at us when we are talking to them.

If people find you overbearing, I can bet your eye contact is part of the problem. If you look too long and don't break away enough, it's intimidating. You want to gaze, not stare. If you gaze more than that 70 percent of the time, people are going to think you're a bully, you're weird or that they have spinach between their teeth.

Gaze is powerful

The six muscles that work together to move each of our eyeballs are common to all vertebrate animals. The muscles' nerves link to unconscious as well as to thinking parts of our brain. We consciously control where our own eyes hover and land, but our eyes have some primal hard wiring as well that make them look at things that are interesting, especially faces. We tend to look away from ugly or distasteful things. We look down or away as part of our primal wiring, as an intense gaze could signal a desire to attack. Numerous studies have shown that unwavering gaze in primates evolved as a sign of dominance and threat, while gaze avoidance evolved as a submissive cue. That's why we face towards the doors in elevators. It would be uncomfortable to break into a fistfight on the fourth floor.

Making eye contact is the most powerful way of establishing contact with another person. As Oprah uses "Make the Connection" for her diet plan, I have been saying for years, "Make eye contact" to make the connection to the other person. Think of eye-to-eye contact as an electric cord; unless you plug into the other person, there is no charge between you. You are working without electricity. Your mouth is moving but they can't and won't hear you.

I love dating. But many years ago, one particular date was not so great. It was a blind date, and it fit the proverbial prediction — it was bad. The guy was yapping away about his business plans, his famous clients, how often he worked out, the new car he was going to buy, etc. I knew that bragging is one of the number one signs a man is interested in you (take my dating workshop for more hints) but I was not interested in him or anything he was saying. So I did not make eye contact — none at all. I was trying to indicate politely that he wasn't connecting. He did not get the hint. His monologue went on and on. I would try to change the subject to something we could both talk about, but he kept going like some pre-recorded message phone pitch. He wasn't just rambling because he was nervous, his voice and body language were actually cocky. He was just clueless. He managed to talk for three hours without my making eye contact with him. He didn't find out a single thing about me. Make the connection!

Making the connection is critical in our evaluation of speakers on television. I analyzed all the Bush-Kerry debates during the election of 2004 for various media outlets. I believe one of the nonverbal effects that most dramatically affected Kerry during the debates was his lack of eye contact with the camera. He made the connection with the moderator — one vote — instead of the camera, which would have made him appear to be making eye contact with all of us. It was a critical mistake that made him look less friendly and less honest.

Even children know

We teach children to make the connection with eye contact and they quickly learn its benefits.

When my nephew, Chris was born, our family would gather in any room where he was and look at him, play peek-a-boo with him and generally gaze into his baby blues with what our family now fondly calls "baby worship." Now Chris is grown with a baby of his own. And we repeat what we did when Chris was born; we all gladly sit on the floor, bow down and coo to Edwin's big blue eyes.

Chris's son, Edwin, loves this. He lights up, his mouth drops open, and he laughs. It's great. Everywhere we go, whether restaurants, the drug store or walking down the street, people stop to give baby worship to little Edwin. Recently, Chris went with his wife and the six-month-old Edwin to California, which required two long plane trips.

"Patti, it was the funniest thing. We would get on the plane, Edwin would be smiling and he would try to make eye contact with the people around us. They wouldn't look at him. He would try and try but no matter where he looked, people would look down and away. They were probably thinking, 'Oh God. I am sitting near a baby who is going to be crying for the next four hours!'" Edwin got frustrated. He was used to making the connection and nobody would give him his well-deserved baby worship.

Here's an interesting fact: From birth, human infants prefer to look at faces that are looking at them. Two-to-five-day old babies discriminate between direct and averted gaze. We start loving mutual gazes early. Healthy babies show more activity in the brain when given a direct gaze than a glance. Some researchers theorize that if you play with your baby in games of mutual gaze you help grow the baby's brain.

Pediatricians say to increase a baby's ability to make eye contact, you can wave your hands in front of your eyes, wear funny eye makeup or big, clown- like false eye lashes or funny glasses to direct the child to look at you in the eyes. You can give an extra big smile when the child gives you direct eye contact or you can give them a toy or small bit of soft candy if they are old enough to chew. Most importantly, make the eye connection with your baby. After all, you may be preventing your child from being a bad blind date.

GAZING

I have mentioned that I used to train all branches of law enforcement officers. I noticed that that they all had very intent eye contact, so I started asking them about it.

Many said that they found they had trouble in social settings where people did not know them. They tended to make other people uncomfortable because their gaze was a little too long and too intense. They said that this is one of the reasons they tend to hang out with each other. My participants who were undercover cops said they had to be careful to turn off their "laser" looks so they wouldn't blow their cover. There was a distinct advantage in their ability to look people straight in the eye. When they gave speeches in my class, they made great eye contact with everybody!

Here are some ways we make eye contact, how you can use them, and how they affect the way others view you.

Mutual Eye Contact

Mutual eye contact arouses our emotions. Our breathing rate and our heart rate go up and if maintained for too long, our palms sweat. Normal, mutual eye contact rarely lasts longer than three seconds before one or both people have the urge to break the contact by glancing down or away. Breaking eye contact lowers our stress levels. Eye-to-eye contact with dilated (large) pupils and a normal blink rate means they are interested in what you are saying, and probably like and admire you.

Upper Triangle Gaze

In business conversation, you should be focused mainly on the other person's eyes. A trick to look powerful or to maintain control is to keep your eyes in the triangle of their eyes and the area just above the bridge of their nose and not let your gaze go lower.

Middle Triangle Gaze

In everyday interpersonal conversation, you should look at the mouth at its base and the nose at its peak. But if you typically use that as your only focus triangle and don't ever look at the upper triangle, you'll look submissive.

Bottom Triangle Gaze

This is a large triangle going from the eyes all the way down to the center of the chest. Let's say you're negotiating with someone and your eyes drop from the upper triangle and stay on the chest of your fellow negotiator as they say a certain point. You may be sending a signal that you're willing to give on that point. The bottom gaze looks like a sign of submission. In Japan, listeners are taught to focus on a speaker's neck in order to avoid eye contact.

Culturally, there are significant differences in acceptable gaze location focus and length. In most cultures, you can gaze above the neck and below the knees. Gazing too long in the middle of those two areas sends an inappropriate sexual signal.

Blinking

Our normal blinking rate is 20 closures per minute. If someone blinks even slightly more than that, it can be a sign he or she is excited or nervous. We are symbolically protecting ourselves from the stressful situation. In fact, blinking is like a polygraph test of our arousal. The excitement causes the brain to release dopamine and that makes us blink faster. Our blinks naturally rise with anxious or tense topics.

The blink rate when you're relaxed is 10 to 20 blinks per minute. When you're talking, it increases to about 20 to 25 blinks per minute. As a blink rate climbs above 50, and especially when it gets above 70, it indicates an increased level of stress.

I was interviewed on FOX News with Neal Cavuto. I was in a studio with an earpiece in my ear. I was studying a monitor on my right to analyze the body language of a politician and trying to remember to look at the camera so it would appear that I was talking to Neal. It was a real "pat your head, rub your tummy at the same time" exercise. I ran home excited to see the tape of the interview. It wasn't good. Each time I gave an answer that was too long for TV, Neal would jump in and interrupt me and I would blink like a house afire. If that was not embarrassing enough, I sent out my own bad signals! As I mentioned that increased blink rate could signal deception, I started blinking faster! I have since learned to shorten my answers to appropriate sound bite length, and thankfully stopped blinking.

Increased blinking is a common occurrence. When someone appears before a television camera, blink frequency increases to 30 to 50 times a minute because of "audience stress."

Blinking slowly so the eyes are closed for up to a second signals everything from disinterest to superior attitude to boredom. Rapid blinking signals disbelief, lack of acceptance and occasionally attraction or nervousness.

Eyelash Flutter

Former President Richard M. Nixon gave his resignation speech on television and appeared calm, cool, and collected. But he showed episodic bursts of blinking above the normal 50 bpm cut-off. This rapid blinking during stress is called the "Nixon effect" or eyelash flutter.

In eyelash flutter, the eye doesn't close completely and flutter is incredibly fast. In TV interviews and police interrogations, this is a sign the flutterer is uncomfortable with the question and they know they have to lie. In training trail lawyers and mediators, I suggested they give witnesses or clients several choices similar to what happened. When they see the person's eyes flutter, they have the true answer.

Researcher J. J. Tecce of Boston College found that "...of the seven (U.S.) presidential elections for which televised debates are available, in six elections the candidate who blinked the most frequently during debates eventually lost the election. In the seventh election, that of 2000, the faster blinker (George W. Bush) lost the popular vote but won the electoral vote." Gore blinked less in the debate but looked down frequently, and had double blinks, and blink bursts of three per second or more." In the first Bush-Kerry debate, Tecce found that Bush blinked less 95 percent of the time.

Tip: If someone likes what they see, their pupil size increases and so does their blink rate. When you want someone to know you like them, and you want them to feel more excited around you, try increasing the blink rate of the person you're talking to. Blink more yourself. If the person likes you, they'll unconsciously try to match your blink rate to keep in sync with you, which in turn, makes you both feel more attracted to each other!

Sideways Glances

Sideways glances need to be examined along with other cues. If someone gives you a sideways glance, looks up and smiles, they may be saying, "Hey baby, I am interested" or simply showing they are happy. This is different from the involuntary eye movements to the right or left that we do when we are processing information.

Eye Rub

When you rub your eyes, it indicates lack of comfort or deceit. If someone rubs their eyes and then looks down and away, it's a strong sign they are lying. If they do it when you are talking, they may not believe you. It also can show a lack of comfort with the topic as in "I wish to 'see no evil'" so I will rub my eyes.

Eye Roll

An eye roll is a dismissive gesture that indicates superiority.

You have may have heard about NLP techniques that say where someone looks — up or down and to the right or the left — tells you're what they are thinking. What you may not know is that the least intimidating way to break eye contact in a good conversation is to break and look down. Just notice how you tend to break eye contact. Breaking by looking down shows submission, it's not going to make you look powerful, but it will make people feel more comfortable around you and increase their self-disclosure.

Staring

Being stared at arouses the sympathetic nervous system and can make the fight-or flight response kick in. A stare with large pupils can mean the person wants to attract you or just plain wants you. We usually think of eye contact as showing interest, but a particular type of eye contact, an unblinking stare with contracted (small) pupils, means the person is actually not interested in what you are saying and/or they don't agree with your views.

> *Tip: You're standing there talking to your husband. He is saying "un huh, un huh" but continues to stare at the television. Looking away doesn't always mean, "I am not listening." As a gender, men can focus on the conversation and not be making eye contact. Guys, I know you're going to take this page and show it to your wives, but just because you have those special powers does not mean that you shouldn't look when your sweetie is talking to you.*

Looking away or closing your eyes while listening can occasionally be helpful, as it can keep you from being distracted by visual stimulation that would not be helpful. Just as I have noticed that adults with ADD will cross their arms to focus, listen and close down distractions, I have noticed that people over the age of 65 and people who have slight hearing problems will look away to listen.

> *Tip: The eyes of someone who is lying meet ours less than 30 percent of the time, but lack of eye contact does not necessarily mean you are lying. A liar can look you straight in the eye. Paul Ekman says in his classic work, Telling Lies: Clues to Deceit in the Marketplace, Politics, and Marriage, "When we asked people how they would be able to tell if someone were lying, squirming and shifty eyes were the winners. If the clue is something everyone knows about, that involves behavior that can be readily inhibited, it won't be very reliable if the stakes are high and the liar does not want to be caught." In fact, of the five types of liars, the scariest ones to misinterpret, the pathological liars, are great at making eye contact.*

> *Tip: To make a woman more comfortable, try to keep your eye contact site line lightly below hers. That means look slightly at the middle gaze triangle I mentioned previously. This is critically important if you're a man trying to make a woman with less power feel important or more at ease. Straight eye-to-eye contact can seem too aggressive. I told this to a journalist who was doing a story on flirting cues. He called back later to tell me it worked so well that he had a date that Saturday!*

When speaking one-on-one, maintain eye contact with your partner by looking from one eye to the other, not with the swinging regularity of a metronome, but as though you were planting a message in each eye. This not only will make your eyes sparkle, but will touch the listener and make you appear sincere.

Bold print body language

When we type an e-mail to a friend, we may bold print a word to show we really mean it, that the word is really important. We use our voice and gestures to emphasize words as well, but a more subtle cue to look for is the widening of the eyes when a particular word is spoken. This cue acts as non-verbal italics or bold print for the words. Blinking can also be a similar indicator. If you watch someone carefully, you'll see him or her blink at the start or end of an important word. This gives the word a special stress.

Cut-off Greeting Eye Contact

The next time you're at a party, notice how people greet, embrace and then step back and look away. Anthropologist Adam Kendon calls this "the cut-off." He believes it's a way of maintaining equilibrium when neither of us has power over the other. Think about how there is a certain acceptable level of touch, hug length time and mutual gaze when you greet your friends and acquaintances. It's based on the level of intimacy you have with each other. If you don't follow this little ritual, if you look at each other too long, it feels uncomfortable. Some kind of cut-off is needed afterward so that everything can quickly get back to normal.

> *Tip:* When you are listening to coaching and feedback as well as criticism, it is normal to want to break eye contact and look down. Instead, maintain normal look/look away eye contact. It makes you look confident and professional and according to research is likely to shorten the length of the criticism because the speaker knows you are listening to and accepting the information.

Gaze Down

This look can mean defeat, reflect guilt, shame, or submissiveness. In fact, when we are startled, gazing quickly down is part of reflexive response. In interrogation or when answering on the witness stand, police officers and lawyers look for where the gaze of the suspect goes as they profess to be innocent. If they say, "I am innocent" and immediately glance down and away, the suspect is not confident of his own innocence. We tend to hold our gaze at normal face-to-face level and hold the gaze for three seconds or longer when telling the truth. Take the famous, "I did not have sexual relations with that woman…" speech of former President Clinton. His first response after finishing that statement was to gaze down. The gesture cluster around that statement also included an immediate gaze down, a finger point, clenched lips, and a swallow, and as he left the podium, a tongue thrust.

Narrowed Eyes

Suddenly narrowed or slitted eyes may reveal disagreement or uncertainty. Our brains are actually protecting us from the pain or discomfort of hearing a disagreeable message by a quick tightening of the eye that hides the eye under lowered hoods.

In research on eye contact in job interviews, researchers found that candidates with nonassertive eyes (defined as averted, downcast, teary, or pleading) or aggressive eyes (identified as narrowed, cold, or staring) were rated significantly lower than candidates with assertive eyes (open, frank, and direct).

The Eyebrow Flash

When we first see someone we're attracted to, our eyebrows rise and fall. If they are similarly attracted, they raise their eyebrows in return. Never noticed? It's not surprising, since the whole thing lasts only about a fifth of a second!

Exercise

Go back to my candidates from the beginning of the chapter. Reassess your choice and see if the information you have just learned changed your mind!

Conclusion

How I Became a Body Language Expert

PEOPLE ALWAYS ASK ME HOW I BECAME A BODY LANGUAGE EXPERT. Your life history forms you. Every seemingly insignificant period of your life makes you who you are. I know that my experiences from childhood on have shaped and formed my interpretative abilities.

When I was six months old, my family moved to Germany and lived there until I was four. During the day, I was left with a German-speaking nanny. As I grew older, I was sent to a German kindergarten. Subsequently, while my family spoke English, my first language was German. In the evening when my family tried to communicate with me in English, it sounded like gibberish. So I read their body language. Thus, my life as a watcher began. I watched and listened to all the people around me. I was able to "read" people, understand them and know them in ways that other people didn't. But I couldn't seem to explain to grownups what I saw.

Then when I was in fourth grade, my teacher taught us how to write poetry, and I finally had a way of putting on paper what I saw and heard in a way that didn't make people uncomfortable. Every day from fourth grade until my sophomore year of college, I watched people and wrote the about the secrets I saw in poetry. I filled large journals at night and carried small notebooks with me during the day. I would write while in my sleeping bag at sleepovers, or while I dripped dry at pool parties, or stood against the wall at dances. I wrote on the back of church bulletins in the choir loft and sitting on the church bus on our youth group trips. I grew up watching and writing, painting my world in words.

When I was 15, my sister Jan gave me her old guitar and I played until I grew calluses on the tips of my fingers. Now I took what I saw and sang about it. Sitting on my princess four-poster bed (ordered from the Sears Roebuck catalog), I sang for three hours every night.

During the week, I took drama classes and joined the little theater. My ability to mimic others' body language and take on others' emotions grew. And in between, I read. I devoured three or four books a week. Authors wrote about the lift of an eyebrow and the turn of a head. They must see what I saw, too, I realized. I wondered why they were the only ones who talked about it. I read so many books that the librarians in both junior high and high school insisted I become a school library assistant. They all said that I had read more books than any other student had. In fact, I was a nerd. I was skinny and stringy-haired. I had braces and large brown-framed glasses. Because I knew I was a nerd and there was not a chance in hell of ever being cool, I embraced my nerdiness.

I stood out in the preppy sea of girls in their blue skirts with white sailor blouses and Etienne Aigner belts. I wore bright-colored, hand-made dresses and purposely wore unmatching socks. I didn't smoke in the bathroom, drink at parties, or kiss on dates. I didn't date at all. I read, did things with my church friends and wrote songs and poetry. And day after day, I watched. By the time I went off to college my journals and notebooks filled a box.

In college, I majored in poetry, was president of the music dorm and became a little sister to the music fraternity. My destiny was certain. I would move to New York after college and live in Greenwich Village. There I would sit on a stool in smoky coffeehouses and sing my folk songs like Carole King and Judy Collins. During the day, I would write my lyrics for Broadway shows. But my first poetry class was filled with depressed people. They seemed so lost and lonely. They did not see the world I saw.

I stopped writing. Now I felt lost, too. My sophomore year I was looking at the college course catalog and saw an interesting course listed in the speech department. "Oral Interpretation of Poetry." Famous poetry. Other people's poetry. I could talk about other people's poetry. I signed up for the class. The class was wonderful so I changed my major to interpersonal and organizational communication, and I was lucky enough to take a nonverbal communication class. The first day of class as the teacher talked, I had a life changing Eureka moment. I realized that all these years that is what I had been seeing — nonverbal communication. This was the secret world I could not seem to explain in anything but poetry and song. As a "watcher", I had been reading people for years, and now I was able to break down into cues what lead to my intuitions about people.

That summer I worked as a substance abuse counselor because I thought that counseling would be a great way to help others. It was awful. My fellow counselors were wonderful and admirable people, but the clients struggled to recover. My mentor said all of her clients from when she first started were cycling back. She was so discouraged she quit. I had trouble not taking my clients' pain home at night. Even though it was a tough experience, I am grateful I had the opportunity to work as a counselor because it made me realize I wanted to help people prevent that kind of pain.

As I worked toward my undergraduate and eventually my master's degree and later in my doctoral coursework in interpersonal communication with an emphasis in nonverbal communication, I took courses and did research in the topics I would eventually speak about.

In my master's degree program, I studied with Larry Barker, the country's leading guru on nonverbal communication. He was also the author of a book on listening. He had a big shelf in his office of books that he had authored or co-authored. I was very nervous the night before my first presentation in his class. I remembered what my boyfriend told me once. "You're nervous because you rehearse your failure, and what you rehearse, you will play out." So I sat in my office and rehearsed my success. In my mind's eye, I wowed Dr. Barker.

The next day, after my lecture, Dr. Barker said, "You were meant to be a speaker." He got me a gig lecturing to the Alabama Speakers Association. And professors there said, "You were meant to be a speaker." The same sentence grew in power. Why those exact words?

I taught college over the years and got incredible joy being with my students week after week and seeing their curiosity and excitement grow. I felt a genuine obligation to nurture them. What a gift those eleven years of college teaching were. I got to be wild and crazy in the classroom. In fact, my college students' short attention spans required that I do things differently. I ran all over the lecture hall, played music that was thematically tied to my lectures each day. I brought in props, played games, blew bubbles and performed live theater. Each class was a chance to make magic with the students.

Each semester in my nonverbal communication class, I had everyone dress wildly punk for a day. That meant my one hundred and fifty students dressed up and went out to the rest of the campus and the town. Then they came to class dressed in their unconventional outfits and talked about it. I remember one semester one of my students, who normally wore punk all the time, chose to wear a suit and tie that day. He took out all his studs and safety pins and wore a friend's loafers instead of army boots and dyed his hair back from purple to brown. He said it was weird to see how people treated him. He said that he had become antagonistic and cynical because day after day people treated him horribly. Now, after going "straight" he realized that he was creating an antagonistic world for himself, a place where he could be mad and where he had an excuse to be mad.

Incidents like this inspired me. I was doing research on everything from sexual harassment and touch in the workplace to mirroring and what makes us liked.

People in the community found out about my college class and asked me to come speak to their businesses. Then I started doing training for different branches of law enforcement. If you have ever spoken in front of a really tough audience, imagine speaking to a room full of men wearing world-weary expressions and guns.

I established my own speaking business, Communication Dynamics, more than twenty years ago. Sometimes early in my career, I was discouraged. People did not believe "body language" was a real science. I spent the first eight years of my career convincing my audiences of its validity so they would begin to explore how nonverbal communication could be useful in their lives. I was not always respected in the universities where I taught or by corporations where I spoke. I was the "touchy feely body language lady." But I kept on doing research and writing and speaking and, of course, watching.

And in spite of initial skepticism, my business grew rapidly. I now deliver more than 100 presentations a year — designing and conducting keynote speeches, workshops and convention seminars for hundreds of companies and national associations. I have trained professionals from many of the world's top corporations in reading body language and have trained top executives from Price Waterhouse, Hewlett Packard; Ripley's Believe It or Not Museums and Porsche on how to form positive first impressions. I've also trained managers, sales personnel, engineers, customer service representatives and financial officers from companies as diverse as Old Navy/The Gap, The Kroger Corporation, Coldwell Banker, United Group Insurance and McGraw-Hill, Merck and Eli Lily; Nortel and Nextel; AT&T Bell South and Lucent Technologies; Chick-Fil-A, Habitat for Humanity and Penske Truck Leasing. In addition, I provide one-on-one coaching for professionals from a number of corporations. I've been able helped law enforcement officers hone their abilities to read deception cues in interviews and interrogations; and lawyers from Coca-Cola, judges and court personnel to read body language for negotiations and courtroom behavior.

And it's not all about business. One of my most rewarding experiences was teaching foster parents how to read the body language of children for signs of depression and abuse. I have also taught single people how to flirt and look for a good mate and coached married couples, teaching them how to watch and listen to their mates and children.

These days body language is a buzzword, and nearly everyone realizes how important understanding it is for total communication. Now companies seek out experts such as myself to help them understand the needs and desires of their consumers and to communicate with the public. I've been a national spokesperson for Wrigley's Spearmint Gum, Benadryl and Vaseline Intensive Care in their efforts to entertain and educate consumers. And national newspapers and magazines such as *The Washington Post, US Weekly, Cosmopolitan, YM, Women's World* and others call on me to analyze photos of politicians and celebrities to help their readers find out more about the people who intrigue them.

Sometimes I've been asked by the broadcast media to help interpret a message given by a political leader. Understanding the nonverbal message that accompanies a verbal message adds an extra layer of meaning to what the person is saying.

Reading body language is an art with a solid basis in sound science. I'm grateful to be able to do what I love for a living. Teaching others this fascinating tool through seminars, workshops and now through my book gives me the greatest pleasure. If you've read this book or even parts of this book, you now have an added insight into the behavior of those around you, and you can use your new knowledge to move forward, sending out the right signals that will lead you to even greater success in your life.

About the Author

PATTI WOOD, MA, CSP, is an international speaker and trainer. Since 1982, she has spoken to hundreds of top companies and national associations. Clients include: AT&T, GTE, Chick-Fil-A, Dupont, Elli Lilly, Merck Pharmaceuticals, Lucent Technologies, The Kroger Company, Nortel Networks, Price Waterhouse, Nextel, Hewlett Packard, and hundreds more. She is on the faculty of Kennesaw University and does training for several other universities including the Wharton School of Business. She delivers more than 100 presentations a year. She is a Certified Speaking Professional.

Called "The Babe Ruth of Body Language" by *The Washington Post,* she is interviewed frequently by the media, including CBS and ABC, FOX News, E! Entertainment, the BBC, PBS, The Discovery Channel, Primetime, *Entrepreneur Magazine,* Reuters, UPI, *Woman's World,* Cosmopolitan, *The Washington Post, Twist, Seventeen, Redbook, Cosmo Girl, J*-14, *The National Examiner, YM, First for Women,* and *Expert Magazine. Time Magazine* recognized her nonverbal communication course at FSU. She is a communication consultant for *US Weekly* and is featured twice monthly. She is a contributing author to several books on interpersonal communications and public speaking. Her research on nonverbal communication led to her position as the National Spokesperson for Wrigley's Spearmint Gum and for Benadryl.

To learn more, visit her website at http://www.pattiwood.com.

SOME OF PATTI'S PROGRAMS

Success Signals — Body Language in Business

Would you like to change your power and confidence through a simple shift in body language? Would you like to have the winning edge in sales and negotiations? Eye blinks to head tilts, palms up to leg locks, this program teaches you how to read and use body language and will help you gain and maintain excellent customer relationships.

Reach Out — Communication That Transforms

When was the last time you had a conversation that affected you profoundly? What are you saying to people that can influence them in a positive way? Do you feel that people are paying attention to what you have to say? In this motivational program, rich with stories and laughter, you will learn ways to communicate and to transform by establishing meaningful rapport, uncovering connecting commonalities, and developing methods to be more open and receptive to others.

Creating and Organizing Powerful Presentations

You will complete this workshop with both the knowledge and the skill to exude confidence to create, organize, and deliver an audience-focused presentation. You will learn how to "wow" your audience and how to keep the needs of your clients in mind while maintaining a high level of creativity. Your presentations will be well structured with strong attention-getters and powerful conclusions and a balance of humor, stories, and pertinent examples tucked in the body. You will learn how to use your body language and read the body language of your audience. You will have the tools to take your presentations to the next level.

Also: Body Honesty and Deception; First Impressions; Dealing With Difficult People and more.

Patti's Clients Speak

Patti stands out above the rest ...
Patti stands out above the rest. I have never seen anyone create the interaction and full participation of every single audience member or create the bonding, energy and results that Patti has achieved in every single program she conducted for us.

— *BMG Distribution*

Dynamic, high energy ...
Patti presented so easily and got everyone committed. It was wonderful! A fantastic job! I was amazed to see the transformation of the participants. Patti is the most dynamic, high-energy presenter I've ever seen. Excellent!

— *GenCorp*

WOW!
Wow! J&J Industries was very impressed with Patti's presentation. How many speakers are asked to come back next year before they even leave the stage?

— *Tarkenton Speakers Bureau*

Superb!
Wow! Superb! Outstanding! Patti never fails to deliver an outstanding program ... In Patti's unique way she provides a dynamic and motivational presentation. She is always committed to giving the audience a meaningful learning experience.

— *American Association of Occupational Health Nurses*

Thought-provoking ...
Informative ...Thought-provoking ... Enjoyable. Patti is a truly fine speaker.

— *GTE*